JEWISH FOLK TALES

IN BRITAIN AND IRELAND

JEWISH FOLK TALES
IN BRITAIN AND IRELAND

LIZ BERG

For my children and grandchildren

'I'm impressed with the easy-going style you have.' – Harvey Kurzfield

First published 2020

The History Press
97 St George's Place, Cheltenham,
Gloucestershire, GL50 3QB
www.thehistorypress.co.uk

British Library Cataloguing in Publication Data.
A catalogue record for this book is available from the British Library.

ISBN 978 0 7509 9143 8

Typesetting and origination by The History Press
Printed and bound in Great Britain by TJ International Ltd.

CONTENTS

FOREWORD

From generation to generation the Jewish people have been great storytellers and passed on tales of everyday life, each sharing the colour, content and narrative, some even an expansion across those generations.

At the core of this tradition is the people's own story of their wanderings contained in the five books of Moses (The Old Testament), the telling of which word for word has remained a central tenet of the Synagogue service on each Sabbath the year round. At the conclusion of each of the five books, the scroll is held aloft and in acknowledgement of their own history, those present cry aloud the Hebrew for 'With strength! With strength roll the story on!' both as a pride in knowing their history and the hopeful continuation of the faith.

Over the centuries since the destruction of the temple in Jerusalem the nature of Jewish storytelling has been carried by the people eastward along the Silk Road, westward through North Africa, up into Italy and Spain, Portugal, France, Germany, England and on into Central and Eastern Europe. Each of these cultures have at one time or another produced a Jewish language and culture of historical expression. Jüddish Deutsch, the language of the Ashkenazi Jews, is known better as Yiddish and is a source of great humour and emotional pathos. Judeo Espagnole and Ladino are the languages of the Sephardi Jews of Spain, Portugal, parts of North Africa and later the Balkans. The names of these groups are taken from the biblical descendants of Noah. So you see, even that is part of the ongoing story.

Like many other countries, England has seen the Jews come and go a number of times, but stories translate understanding as they offer a shared experience. Some of the sources behind these stories may have started elsewhere, but the foibles of humanity are world-wide. Perhaps only the geography changes?

A twist of humour has always been part of the Jewish story-teller's art, as has been the rare gift of healing a hurt through tears and laughter. Even today those of us who call ourselves community storytellers are still here to bind the broken heart of a bereavement, and your smile into a guffaw, and your guffaw into a rolling belly laugh.

The glitter here between the covers is a jewel box of sharing.

A minute of your time perhaps? The hour that we have … to begin with … There's this story.

Now read on and enjoy! Enjoy!

Del Reid
Jewish cultural historian
Mentsch

INTRODUCTION

When I told someone I was writing a book of Jewish folk tales in Britain, they laughed and questioned, 'Is there such a thing?' Then I explained what I meant: not only stories grown here, but brought here in the successive waves of immigration since Roman times. 'Ah,' they said, 'of course.'

It was clear to me what I wanted to do, but not always clear to those I needed to tell me stories – stories their elders brought with them and either told as they were or changed around a little to fit the places they found themselves in. I wanted to give a voice to those communities who were disappearing before my eyes. There are far more cities and towns settled by Jews than I have space to include here.

Some tales were definitely historically linked to a town or city. Others have, through oral storytelling, gained a place that wasn't theirs in the first place. But that is true of all immigrants. We change the stories to fit our present and sometimes change our past to fit our future.

In this constantly changing flow of ideas of what makes a people, I think it is pertinent to tell the stories of the Jewish people in Britain. I remember friends of my parents who had numbers tattooed on the inside of their arms. I often wondered as a small child, why? As Jews we are not allowed to tattoo our skin, and it was both the man and the woman! No one talked about it. I knew enough not to ask, not then, not them. Of course, I learned later about the Holocaust, the concentration camps, and the death camps.

My siblings and I are second generation Welsh. Our parents were both born in Wales and though three of my grandparents were born in Eastern Europe, the Russian Pale of Settlement that included Lithuania, Poland and Ukraine and came in during the 1880–1900 wave, my maternal grandmother was also born in Wales to a family that had come to Devonport in the 1840s. Four generations British on one side. Four generations who have not had a suitcase packed by the bed in case they were thrown out again. My own children and grandchildren add to the length of time we have been settled here and being British is part of our identity. As a young girl I started to research Jewish communities, learning stories and tales as I went. Through *cheder* I heard more tales from the *Tanakh*, from the *Talmud*. I was hooked.

This book isn't a book of anti-Semitic tales. Goodness knows there are enough of them, especially in areas of Britain where Jews haven't been a presence for more than eight hundred years. How these stories are held in the folk memory and why are different research questions. It is not a book of tales about the Jews from a non-Jewish perspective. Again, this type proliferates in 'literary' writing. It is, however, a book of Jewish memory. Tales, songs and jokes of Jews by Jews told in Britain and Ireland. Jews can tell the same tales all over Britain and adapt them to their landscapes or not. What is important is the story.

As the Dubno Maggid said when asked how his stories were always exactly what his listeners needed to hear, 'Let me tell you a story.

'A young prince was the greatest archer in the kingdom. He won every contest going. He was proud of his achievement. One day he was out riding and happened upon a ramshackle cottage. No wall was the same height as another, the roof was higgledy-piggledy. He would have ridden by if he hadn't noticed targets painted on the walls of the cottage and in the centre of every target was an arrow.

'The prince was amazed. Some of the targets would have been difficult for him, let alone an inferior archer. He called out. A young lad came out. The prince asked him if his parents were home.

'No,' answered the lad.

'Well,' asked the prince, 'did your father shoot these arrows?'

'No,' answered the lad.

'Your mother?'

'No,' answered the lad.

'Don't tell me you did?' asked the prince.

'No,' answered the lad.

'Then who did?' asked the prince, understandably frustrated.

'The lad disappeared behind the cottage and emerged holding the hand of a little girl of about four. The prince watched as the little girl took up her wooden bow and arrow and shot at the cottage walls. As soon as her arrow landed, her brother fetched a pot of paint and painted the target around it, the arrow now firmly in the centre.'

'And that is how my stories are,' said the Dubno Maggid. 'I send them out but you hit the target.'

I have heard this one brought up to date with a sharpshooter in the Austrian army without the Dubno Maggid. Same tale, different landscape, told both times by Jews in Britain.

Sometimes I have attributed stories to certain areas without the certainty that these tales were the exact ones told there, reasoning that these types of stories would, on the side of probability rather than possibility, be told there, for example, tailoring stories in the Leeds area. I have put a story told by the people from that community, for example, German, Iranian or Sephardi, where those communities settled in Britain. If I attribute a story to a country it is the Jewish population of that country who tell the tale, for example, if I state a tale comes from Germany, it is a tale told by German Jews not by the population as a whole, and so on. Jewish tales are Jewish tales and are still being told, transmuted and translated into the idiom of today. For us it doesn't matter that they were told in Russia, Afghanistan, China, Argentina or Australia – the *Torah*, the Bible and the *Talmud*, the Oral Torah, hold stories that shine as much now as they did for our forebears. We set them where we feel comfortable. I have included some personal stories and I am grateful to my individual contributors for allowing me to use them.

I am grateful especially to Sue Field, who supported me every step of the way, encouraging me to write this book and reading each story for me; Del Reid, who shared his wonderful breadth and depth of knowledge of our history with me; the elders in the Stapely Care home in Liverpool, both residents and volunteers, who shared their experiences of growing up in the Liverpool area; and those of Heathlands Village, Manchester, who also shared their experiences and tales. I found connections I hadn't believed possible.

Although I am not expecting this to be, nor should you, an examination of Jewish practices for the uninitiated, I hope that the stories stand with the briefest of explanation. Before each section of tales, I have added a succinct history of the Jewish community in the area and Jewish rites within the history or tales where necessary. In the glossary you will find an explanation of foreign words as well as an expansion on Jewish ritual mentioned in the stories.

How to transliterate words in Hebrew, Yiddish, Ladino? Do I use the modern way of spelling according to YIVO*? Or do I use the old way I grew up with? Should there be a consistent spelling of certain words, for example, *Shabbat, Shabbos, Shabbes* (Sabbath)? Which is right? They all are. It depends on circumstances, which community's tales I am telling. It is completely inappropriate for me to write *Shabbos* when telling a Sephardi tale, or *Shabbat* when retelling an Ashkenazi tale that I haven't brought up to date. (I once had a shock when I heard a North Welsh story told in a South Welsh accent by an English storyteller. It brought me out of the story immediately, so I am doubly wary.) Should I use the modern *kh* for the guttural sound like the *ch* in loch? Although correct, it makes the word look odd to my eyes. I have tried for consistency, but forgive me if I fail in some places. I haven't included a pronunciation guide as, like local accents and dialects, the Jewish way of saying a word can depend on where you are from within Britain, for example, the rolls that are tied like knots are *bulkas, bulkies, bolkies*. Or as a joke has it: There is only one way to spell Christmas. No one can decide how to spell *Chanukah, Chanukkah, Chanukka, Channukah, Hanukah, Hannukah,* etc.

---

* YIVO is the acronym of Yidisher Visnshaftlekher Institut (Yiddish Scientific Institute), now known as YIVO Institute for Jewish Research, a body that among other things preserves the Yiddish language.

Some words are British Yiddish. Is there such a thing? Well, at *Ot Azoy*, the annual week-long Yiddishfest held by the Jewish Music Institute (JMI) in London in August, I was in a conversation class. The subject was what we did in the summer. The woman next to me, Haidee Kenedy, told us in Yiddish about taking her dog out on Hampstead Heath and calling for him. What was the dog's name? *Lobos*, she said. I started laughing. The other participants from France, Finland, USA, Canada and Holland all looked at us. Haidee turned to me and said, 'It's an English Yiddish word. Only the English use it.'

'It was well-used in Wales,' I said. My father used to call the boys a *lobos* if they had misbehaved. It means a scamp, miscreant or rapscallion. Some weeks later I was researching for this book and two people in different parts of the country offered me this little ditty:

The boy stood on the burning deck
His father called him *lobos*
Because he wouldn't wash his neck
Or go to *shul* on *shabbos*.

I hope these Jewish stories lead you to retell them to your children and your children's children. *Ledor vador*. From generation to generation.

Liz Berg, 2020

ILLUSTRATOR'S NOTE

I am a textile artist from Cornwall. I gained a First Class Honours degree in printed textile design from Winchester School of Art and have worked as a freelance designer and college lecturer.

My work is mainly mixed media collage with machine embroidery. I am greatly influenced by the landscape around me and I draw inspiration from the textures and patterns to create my pieces. I manipulate and recycle fabrics, papers and photographs, adding finer detail with machine embroidery and print.

For this collection of work, I was inspired by the concept of the retelling and repetition of folk tales. I love the sense of familiarity created by the recurring themes, even though the stories have been gathered from far and wide, and this was something I wanted to echo in my imagery.

You will see shapes, patterns and textures repeated throughout the illustrations. This hopefully parallels not only the familiarity and rhythm found in the stories, but also the idea of new interpretation – just as stories are re-told and reinterpreted with each telling.

Karen Berg

LONDON

Henry VIII wanted to make his court the best there was anywhere. To do this, he recruited musicians from all over the known world. In the 1540s he established a royal court of musicians, Italian Jewish musicians and instrument makers, who came from Venice with their families. They were allowed in on licence from the king, arranged by Thomas Cromwell, who paid their passage. Some had arrived earlier, like Anthony Moyses, a sackbut player, who had come in 1526. When Anthony was dying, he chose as his executors not the English wind players he had known for sixteen years but the four Italian Jewish viol players he'd only known for eighteen months. The musicians settled initially in London. They relied on royal patronage whilst also dealing in trade, having strong links to Antwerp. Whilst some married within the faith, there were many who married out. The most successful families – the Lupos, Comys and Bassanos – established musical dynasties that dominated Royal music for more than a century.

The Italian Jewish musicians kept away from the other Jews on licence, the Portuguese doctors and lawyers. At one point the Italian Jews lived on one side of the street and the Portuguese Jews on the other in a small village. They didn't mix. At all. They held their own services and the families never spoke. The Portuguese Jews looked down on their fellow Jews as ill-educated paupers.

The musicians settled in St Alphage, Cripplegate, where more Jewish instrument makers joined them, this time from Poland. The Jewish musicians who were recruited were of the best in Europe. They developed the violin, which was unknown before its use by Henry VIII's viol consort. Jewish musicians played a large part in the renaissance of music and some people assert that this viol consort was one of the first in the world.

This is a story collected from Egypt where many Sephardic Jews settled. I like to think that the viol consort might have encouraged the spreading of the tale.

ELIJAH'S VIOLIN

Once there was a king who was on the brink of going to war overseas. He asked his three daughters to name something they wanted him to bring back. His eldest asked for a star-shaped diamond so she could hold the night sky in her hands. His second daughter asked for a gown woven of pure gold so the sun would envy her as she walked. The youngest asked him to come back safely. He laughed and hugged her. 'I was planning on that,' he said. 'Go and think what you would like me to bring back. You have three days before I sail.'

The young princess walked out of the palace and down to her favourite thinking spot on the shore of the lake. Perched on the rock, she stared over the water. Nothing came into her mind that she did not already have.

An old woman came and sat down next to her. 'Why are you so sad?' The princess explained.

'Ah,' said the old woman, 'you must ask him for Elijah's violin.' Then she added in a quiet voice the princess didn't hear, 'It is time for the melodies to be heard.'

The princess thanked her and ran back to her father, who was pleased she had found something she wanted. Amid hugs, kisses and tears of farewell, the king sailed off to war.

Many hard battles later, he was victorious. He set about finding the gifts for his daughters. Before too long he had the star-shaped diamond and the gown of gold. What he didn't have and couldn't find was Elijah's violin. He sent out messengers, who came back empty-handed; he consulted his wise men, who consulted their great tomes to no avail; he sought the seers, who saw nothing in the stars. He set sail, determined to search until he found Elijah's violin and every place they landed he looked for it. Then one day he climbed into a cave where an old man lived.

'Yes,' said the old man. 'Elijah's violin is in the possession of the king of this land. His daughter has been enchanted, imprisoned in stone, and there is a great reward for anyone who can cure her. Take these three strands from the bow of the violin and when you are in the presence of the princess, burn them immediately. Then ask for the violin.'

'Thank you,' said the king as he tucked the three strands away carefully in his pocket. 'What can I give you in return?'

'Nothing. When your daughter plays Elijah's violin she will release all the imprisoned melodies into the world. That will be my reward.'

'What is your name?' asked the king.

The old man smiled. 'Elijah.'

The king and his men travelled quickly to the palace of the king. Outside the walls, the king made camp and said he was going in alone. He was admitted once he said he wanted to cure the princess. He was warned failure meant his death. He gritted his teeth and agreed. Inside the room where the princess stood a fire burned in the fireplace, but no warmth came into the room. The king shivered.

The princess looked for all the world as if she were made of stone. She couldn't move, but astonishingly she could speak. When she spoke, life flowed back into her cheeks. When she stopped, she turned to stone.

'How did this happen?' asked the king.

The princess told of her finding an unknown staircase in the palace one day and following it to the top. Up in the room she found a mirror with a golden frame. As she looked at herself in the mirror, her reflection crept out of the mirror and forced her to change places. Ever since then she had been petrified, turned to stone apart from when she spoke. Reports had come in of her being seen around the country but her reflection had slipped away before anyone had managed to get hold of her.

The king remembered what he had to do. He took out the three strands and threw them on the fire. They burned so brightly that the air in the room warmed immediately. As he watched, life returned to the princess. Flesh and blood took the place of stone.

'Your reflection is back in the mirror,' said the king. 'Blindfold yourself before you enter the room so she doesn't have the chance to do this again. Smash the mirror with a stone. Do it now.'

The princess thanked the king and dashed off to complete the disenchantment.

Her father was overjoyed and asked the king to name his reward.

'Elijah's violin, please,' asked the king.

The violin was handed over with great ceremony.

The king left with his men and sailed back to his own country. They arrived a week later to cheers and tears of relief all round.

His three daughters crowded round him. He gave them their gifts. The elder two ran off with the star-shaped diamond and the gown woven of pure gold straightaway. His youngest kissed him and hugged him. She was so glad he had come back safe and sound. Only then did she go to her room with Elijah's violin.

She opened the case to find a beautifully carved violin nestling inside its plush interior. She lifted it out and took up the bow. As soon as she began to play a wonderful melody started. It was if the violin was playing itself. Melody after melody streamed out of the violin, out of its internal sources.

Suddenly, as the princess continued to play, a handsome young man appeared.

'How did you get here?' asked the princess.

'Through the window,' he answered.

'Where are you from?'

'Far, far away. The music brought me here. I had no choice.'

Soon the princess and the prince, for that was what he was, found they had other things to talk about. Whenever the princess got lonely and missed the prince, she would play the violin and he would appear through the window. They fell in love and exchanged rings, promising to marry.

One day, the eldest sister was passing the room when she heard her sister talking to someone.

'Our sister has a man in her room, I'm sure of it. You distract her and then I can search her room for evidence,' she said to her middle sister.

While the two younger sisters were having a mud massage, the eldest ransacked the princess' room. She found the prince's ring and jealously threw it through the window, breaking the glass. She opened the case and picked up Elijah's violin. The music she played was dark and full of menace. The prince was drawn by the music to the room but as he tried to get through the window, the broken glass cut him and he disappeared. The princess shoved the violin back in its case. Hurriedly, she tidied up and left, frustrated.

Fresh and relaxed from her massage, the princess returned to her room. It felt wrong. Something spoiled. She wanted to speak to the prince and so she played the violin. But he didn't come. She tried again. Nothing. She walked over to the window and saw the broken glass and by the curtain, three drops of blood. She realised the prince must be hurt or worse.

Heartbroken, the princess went down to her thinking spot, the rock by the lake. Not long after, the old woman hobbled up. The princess poured all her woes and worries into the old woman's ear.

'Listen. Do you want to find him?'

The princess nodded.

'Then this is what you must do. Go to your room and have a doctor insist you are too ill to see anyone. Slip out of your room and then begin your search. It might take a long time.'

'I don't care,' said the princess. 'I have to find him and make him well again.'

'Good,' said the old woman. 'Take three strands from the bow of Elijah's violin with you. When you see him, burn the strands in the fire immediately.'

The princess did as she was told. The doctor came and put her under quarantine. She slipped out after taking three strands from the bow of Elijah's violin. She walked and walked. She walked through meadows, she walked through woods, she crossed streams. She was so tired she sat down to rest under an elder tree. As she closed her eyes, about to fall asleep, she heard two doves talking in the branches above her. She opened her eyes and the birds were cooing as usual. She closed her eyes and she understood what they were saying.

'Did you hear about the prince? He's been so badly injured, they think he might die,' said one.

'Yes. It's a shame it's so difficult to get to his palace. More people would try to cure him if they could only find the way,' said the other.

'If only they knew the leaves of this tree are maps to his home,' cooed the first.

The princess shot up and broke off a green leaf. As she stared at it, a map became clear to her. She took new heart and set off with determination. After some time, she arrived at the gates of the palace.

Disguised as a doctor, she knocked for admittance. 'I've come to cure the prince,' she said, and was shown into the throne room where the king and queen sat.

'You do know thirty-nine doctors have tried before you. Each one paid the price for failure. Are you willing to give up your life?' asked the king.

'If I can see his royal highness alone,' answered the princess bravely.

The king agreed and the princess was shown into the prince's bedroom.

He looked so pale and wan lying there, she wanted to rush over and kiss him. But she knew she had something to do first. She took out the three strands and threw them on the fire.

As she watched, his cuts began to heal themselves. Blood rushed to his cheeks and flushed his body. Soon he was awake and looking into her eyes, brimming with tears of gladness. They talked and found they still felt the same as they had done before.

She changed out of her doctor's disguise back into her own clothes and called his parents in. They rushed in, overjoyed at having their son back. They thanked the princess and gladly agreed to the wedding. The pair lived happily and virtuously for all their lives. The melodies from Elijah's violin often floated out into the world from their palace.

Bevis Marks, in the centre of the City of London, is the oldest extant synagogue in Britain. It was founded in 1701 and stands in a secluded courtyard with a stone archway with wrought iron gates. Above the gates are the Hebrew words 'Kahal Kadosh Shaar Hashama'im' meaning 'Holy Congregation, The Gates of Heaven' and expressing gratitude for the safe refuge established by the first Sephardim in the City.

Some of the Sephardim had practised Judaism in secret, celebrating mass in the Portuguese Embassy in London. Their families had been forcibly converted instead of being expelled from Spain in 1492 and Portugal in 1497. These were called Crypto-Jews, hidden Jews or Anusim. There is a further term that is no longer used due to its offensive nature. Others had fled at the same time to the Spanish Netherlands, where after fifty or so years they could practise openly in multi-cultural Amsterdam. Rabbi Menasseh ben Israel negotiated with Oliver Cromwell in 1656 to let the Jews live openly in Britain.

It is said Princess Anne, later Queen Anne, granted the community an oak beam from one of the Royal Navy ships to be incorporated into the roof structure of the first synagogue to be built on British soil for 350 years. The building was designed by Joseph Avis, a Quaker who, it is said, returned to the congregation his profits on the project, saying he wouldn't benefit financially for building a house of God. The synagogue is very atmospheric, especially at night when lit only by the seven many-branched hanging candelabras, representing the days of the week. The seventh in the middle is the largest, being Shabbat.

One of the most famous congregants was Daniel Mendoza, the pugilist. A heavyweight champion whilst at welterweight and only 5ft 7in, his three epic bare-knuckle fights with fellow boxer Richard Humphries have become the stuff of legend. They fought hour after hour to a standstill, until one of them was on the ground. One bout was arranged by the Prince of Wales. Mendoza later opened a boxing club for gentlemen, travelled Britain giving exhibitions, performed at Astleys offering women the science of pugilism without the gore, and acted in pantomime. It was he who instigated the now common sidesteps and movement during a bout. Previously, boxers stood still and traded punches.

This Sephardi story is about hidden depths.

The Sofer and the Donkey

A scholar's wife scolded a man hitting his donkey. The man was incensed that a woman had dared to tell him how to treat his animals. He saw she was pregnant. 'Ha,' he cursed, 'you're so fond of donkeys, let's see how you are with a donkey for a daughter!'

In the fullness of time, a daughter, Losia, was born to the scholar and his wife. They adored her and brought her up happy and loved. As she grew, her quickness of mind proved a delight to her father, who taught her *Torah* and then *Mishnah* and *Gemara*. Soon Losia was making her father think deeper as they studied together. Even though both parents were proud of their daughter, there was a little corner of their hearts filled with sadness. They despaired of ever standing under the *chuppah* with her and her bridegroom. Ever since childhood Losia had been teased and stones thrown at her by ignorant children. She went everywhere heavily veiled. But her voice … her voice was the voice of an angel.

One day a young man walked past the window of the scholar's house. He heard the sound of *pilpel*, pepper, two people studying Torah. He paused to see if the arguments were thorough. He listened and was lost in the girl's voice explaining clearly and sweetly a problem he'd long been puzzling over. He fell in love instantly.

Immediately he rapped at the door. When he explained that he wanted to marry their daughter, the couple were overwhelmed.

'You've never seen her. You may change your mind.'

'I won't change my mind. Her voice shows how beautiful she is. Her learning shows how beautiful she is. I love her and I want to marry her as soon as possible.'

No matter what arguments the parents put forth, he dashed them away as frivolous. Eventually they gave in. They went to their daughter, who had been standing behind the door listening.

'What do you say?'

Losia liked the look of the young man and hoped he was a man of his word. She agreed.

The *chuppah* was set up and the bride came heavily veiled, as was the custom. She walked seven times around the *chatan*, whose heart swelled with love for the clever girl he was marrying. The wine cup was handed to her under her veil. He stamped on the glass and everyone present wished them *mazal tov!*

Not until they were in the bedroom, alone together for the first time, did he attempt to remove her veil. He protested how much he loved her. How he had loved her from the first moment he'd heard her beautiful voice explaining Torah.

'Take off your veil, Losia,' he entreated. 'I will love you whatever you look like.' Secretly he thought anyone with such a beautiful voice and mind couldn't be so bad.

'Promise you will not shame me, Rafael,' said his bride. Her hands trembled as she lifted her veil.

He recoiled in disgust when he saw not a human face looking at him, but that of a donkey! He grabbed his coat, put his hand to the door and was about to leave the room and the marriage. He stopped when he heard his wife's angelic voice, full of tears, asking him to stay, just for the wedding night. When he couldn't see her, his heart was full of love. He turned back to find her veiled once more.

The cruel light of morning twisted Rafael's heart. He couldn't bear to look on her, knowing what lay beneath the veil. He crept out of the room and ran away as far as he could. He ran so fast he left behind his *tallit* (prayer shawl), his *siddur* (prayer book) and his silver ring he'd taken off before he'd said the morning prayers.

Losia went down to her parents and wept. Both her mother and father put their arms around her and comforted her. When she gave birth to a boy, Bonanat, the whole family rejoiced. Bonanat grew and played with the other children. He started coming home, his clothes dirty and torn, with scratches on his body.

'What is it my child, my crown?' asked his mother, hugging him to her.

'Nissim and the others said I don't have a father. And you're a *makshefa*, a witch, because you always wear a veil outside.' The little boy half sobbed. 'But I made them eat their words.'

His mother comforted her son as best she could. There was little she could do. Out of the house she went heavily veiled but inside she could be herself. Her son loved her as she was. Her parents loved her as she was. If she longed for someone else that was for her alone.

She taught her son as her father had taught her. When Bonanat went in front of the rabbi to study for his *bar mitzvah* the following year, the rabbi was astounded at the breadth of his knowledge.

'Who taught you so well, Bonanat?' the rabbi asked.

'My mother,' the boy answered proudly.

From then on, when there was a sticky question, the rabbi referred the questioner to Losia, who seemed to find just the right answer. People accepted that whenever they saw her, she was veiled. That was just how Losia was, they said. What did it matter? The mind, the wisdom, that was the important thing.

But for her son, there was one burning question that his mother couldn't answer. Where was his father? Day after day he asked.

'Why do you want to find him, my crown?' asked Losia.

'To show him what he lost!'

When Bonanat's *bar mitzvah* finally dawned, nobody could have been prouder than Losia and her parents as they watched him read from the Torah scrolls for the first time. Their eyes glistened as they listened to him explain a point from his *sedra*.

Losia knew that she could not deny her son any longer. One night she took out the *tallit, siddur* and silver ring she had kept these past years. She held Bonanat's hand and explained to him what had happened. And, as she knew he would, Bonanat declared his intention of going off to look for his father.

'Be careful, my son, my crown. Return to me, whole in heart.'

Bonanat kissed his mother on her furry cheek and then set off. He had his father's name, profession and description. He was sure he could find him. In his pocket his grandfather had given him promissory notes to exchange on the way as well as a bag of coins. In his pack his grandmother had prepared enough food for several days along with several water bottles. At the bottom of his pack, underneath his change of clothes and his own *tallit* bag and *siddur*, tucked in very carefully, was the velvet bag containing his father's *tallit, siddur* and silver ring.

Bonanat travelled far. At every village and town, he stopped and asked if a man called Rafael lived there. At every village and town, they told him no. He changed the promissory notes with merchants who did business with his grandfather. He spent his coins buying food and a bed for the night wherever he stopped. He was weary but not disheartened. He knew that just one more village or the next town would lead him to his father.

Sof-sof, eventually, Bonanat reached a town where his father's name was known. His spirits lifted. He would find his father! He asked for directions. Rafael was a well-respected *sofer*, a scribe. He had come to this town to finish writing a Torah scroll. Bonanat was thrilled. He joined in the celebrations as the Torah scroll was paraded through the town to the synagogue. He had eyes only for the *sofer*, Rafael. The last letter was inscribed, the scroll held up in its ornate wooden case and *mazal tov*! The room erupted.

Bonanat was giddy with relief. Here was his father. After Rafael had endured the handshaking, the cheek kissing and the thumps on the back, he settled down with a cup of wine in his hand.

'Rafael, the *sofer*?' Bonanat asked.

'Yes. And who might you be? You seem familiar but I can't place you. Perhaps I've had too much to drink.'

Bonanat drew out his father's *tallit, siddur* and silver ring from his pack. He held them carefully out to Rafael.

Rafael blanched. 'Where did you get these?'

'They are my inheritance. They belong to my father. My father who married my mother Losia and left her after the wedding.'

'Losia!' Rafael stared at Bonanat. 'No, you can't be.'

'I am your son, Bonanat.'

'My son, my son,' and Rafael started to weep.

The two talked long into the night and the next day. Bonanat persuaded his father to come back with him, to see his mother.

'She is so beautiful and so wise. People come and ask her questions that even the rabbi can't answer.'

'They do? That's how I fell in love with her in the first place … she answered a question I had been puzzling over.'

They walked and they talked. Rafael grew closer to this son of his, who loved his mother so much. He remembered loving Losia's voice and wisdom before he saw her face. He became remorseful. One night Rafael broke down in tears.

'How I have mistreated your mother! How she has suffered at my hands! If I could make it better, I would. I loved her so much. And yet I was so venial, thinking of myself alone. Oh, if only I could do it over again.'

Bonanat knew not to interrupt this outpouring of sorrow. He patted his father on the shoulder and rolled himself up in his blanket.

That night Bonanat dreamed he was by a river. The current was swift and the water bright. A man stood on the bank of the

river. His face was lit up from within. He held out a sprig of eucalyptus leaves.

'Take these leaves, my son and dip them in the waters from Eden. Bring them back to your mother. Her merit has weighed the scales in her favour. She has suffered enough.'

Bonanat took the leaves from Elijah, for it was he, and dipped them in the fast-flowing waters of the River Gichon. He packed them carefully and looked up to thank Elijah but he had disappeared.

In the morning Bonanat woke up to find a small parcel by his head. He lifted it up to his nose and smelled through the wrapping the fresh scent of eucalyptus. He smiled and thought how pleased his mother would be.

Soon Rafael and Bonanat entered the town where his mother and grandparents lived. Rafael stood outside the same window he had stood outside nearly fourteen years previously. He listened as Bonanat, of whom he was so proud, told Losia and his grandparents of his adventures. Rafael heard his son ask his mother if she was ready to see his father again. Rafael strained but couldn't hear an answer. He hadn't known how much his heart had yearned to hear Losia's beloved voice again. Not hearing a reply, he turned away, saddened and diminished.

'Going so soon, Rafael?'

Her voice acted like water on his parched soul.

He turned to her and fell on his knees begging for forgiveness. 'I was a fool. I caused you so much heartache. Please forgive me. You have the right to divorce me if you wish, I won't contest it. But know that it was your voice and your learning that I fell in love with. I still do, there is no one to match you.'

Losia asked him in. They had much to talk about. She would let him wait a while before she fully allowed him back in her life. He had to show her he was going to stay no matter what.

That night Bonanat brought out the wrapped packet and gave it to his mother. He explained about his dream. Losia smiled faintly. She thought it would do no harm to try. Hadn't her parents tried everything they could when she was young? All to no avail. She

didn't want to disappoint her son whose hope that others would see the beauty he did every time he looked at her, shone so brightly.

She took the eucalyptus leaves, still wet with the waters of Eden, and washed her face with them. She went to bed fragrant.

She was cooking the breakfast when her parents hobbled in. Both looked at her face and then at each other. They burst into tears, sobbing uncontrollably. Losia rushed to comfort them.

'What is it? What's wrong?'

'Your face, your dear face. Blessed be the Source of all creation.'

Together with her parents, Losia poured a bowl of water and looked into it. They saw her face reflected in the surface. Her face was … changed. No more a furry donkey face but beautiful, as beautiful outside as it was shining with the light she held within.

When Bonanat came down he hugged his mother in delight. 'No more veils,' he whispered. And as for Rafael, he couldn't believe his eyes, he blessed his son. The family lived in happiness for the rest of their lives.

Many Jews came to London from the 1800s onward, escaping poverty, pogroms and compulsory enlistment for thirty years in the Tzar's army. They settled around Aldwych and the East End. They lived huddled together in tenements, stinking hovels, many families or bachelors all squashed together. Nobody had money. They made their living buying and selling old clothes that either were sold on or made into paper.

Samuel Taylor Coleridge passed a Jew calling in the most nasal tones for old clothes. Coleridge was provoked into asking why the Jew could not ask for old clothes plainly and clearly just like Coleridge was speaking now. The Jew looked at him gravely and answered in a clear, fine accent. 'Sir, I can say old clothes as well as you. However, if you had to cry it ten times every minute for an hour at a time, all day every day, you would say "Ough Clo" in the same way.' The Jew marched away. Coleridge was floored by the justice of this and ran after him to give him a shilling, the only one he had.

The East End became a hodgepodge of immigrants, among them Italians, Irish, and Jews, over the next hundred years. The streets grew crowded with the life of the poor, trying to finds jobs, make a living.

On Sunday morning in the 1950s and '60s the whole of the north side of Whitechapel was crowded with people from Vallance Road to Black Lion Yard, where the Jewish Tailors' Union head-quarters used to be. Del Reid recalls his walks with his grandfather. The list of jobs available would go up Saturday night, in what was known in Yiddish as the *chazermarkt*; a pig market or hiring fair, just as the manufacturers would do at the docks. 'You want a job? I'll have you and you. Turn up at my factory Monday morning, give me your names.' The tailors stood five to seven deep on the pavements, straining to look at the list and finding a job for the week. Arguments constantly broke out between the taxis, buses and the tailors who spilled out onto the road and stood having conversations with their friends. 'You want me to move? Wait till I've finished talking.'

This story is a well-known one, attributed to Hershel Ostropolier, about the value of clothes.

THE HUNGRY CLOTHES

Leib the merchant had an important guest for *Shabbos*. He invited the men who attended Friday night prayers in the synagogue to come home with him and listen to his guest expound wisdom from the Talmud. As he walked home, Leib was secretly glad the late arrival of the local *schnorrer* in the synagogue meant he hadn't heard him invite everyone to his house. He didn't want to be shown up in front of his fine guest.

The *schnorrer*, Mossy, wondered where everyone was going. Usually he managed to get his Friday night meal by going home with one of the men. Tonight, they all seemed to be heading off to Leib's house.

Mossy hurried after them and knocked on the door. Leib opened the door to him. The merchant looked at Mossy, up and down. He saw the old coat, spotted, stained and ripped. He saw the old shirt, patched, worn and threadbare. He saw Mossy's boots, covered in mud and flapping in places.

'Oh Mossy, what a pity you are so late. I don't have any room left at the table. Never mind. Come next week, a bit earlier so I have a place for you.'

Leib shut the door and hurried back to his important guest.

Mossy sidled to the window. Through the slit in the curtains he saw the table with the men from the synagogue gathered around. He saw, too, there was a chair here and there without an occupant.

Now Mossy wasn't stumped for long. He ran over to his newly married oldest friend and his bride.

He interrupted the Friday night meal and refused to sit down with them.

'Please, do me a favour, lend me your wedding clothes.'

'Well of course, but what do you want them for tonight?' asked his bewildered friend.

'Just help me get dressed and I'll tell you later,' insisted Mossy. 'Hurry, hurry.'

Soon Mossy was knocking on Leib's door again.

The merchant came to the door and looked at Mossy in amazement. His trousers were fine moleskin, his shirt was white and pristine, an embroidered waistcoat strained his stomach, his coat was clean, black with an astrakhan collar and a full set of buttons, his boots were well polished and, to cap it all, he wore a fur *shtreimel* on his head.

'Mossy,' said Leib. 'Where have you been? Come in, come in. I'm sure I can squeeze another chair in for you.'

Mossy smiled and rubbed his hands in anticipation of the meal he would get. His nose could already smell the *gefilte* fish.

'Because you arrived late, we're already on the main course, but you can soon catch up. Sit, sit,' encouraged the merchant.

Mossy sat down and first picked up the plate of *gefilte* fish he had smelled coming in. Nearby was the dish of *chrein*, beetroot and horseradish sauce, to complement the fish. Mossy took two of the fish patties and plopped them into a pocket in his waistcoat. He followed them with a spoonful of *chrein* for each piece of fish. Leib's mouth opened and then closed. He hoped his fine guest hadn't seen what had just happened.

The maid brought in a bowl of chicken soup with *kreplach*, meat-filled pasta parcels, floating in the golden liquid. She put it down in front of Mossy, who promptly picked up the bowl and to the astonishment of the rest of the company, poured the contents down his trousers.

Everyone gaped as Mossy reached for the wine. A glass of ruby red was carefully poured over his pristine white shirt.

But when Mossy stuffed roast chicken into one coat pocket, roast potatoes in another and green salad in his trouser pockets, his host had had enough.

'Stop this nonsense at once Mossy! I invited you in, thinking you were at last acting like a person. You have embarrassed me. Me and my guest! What were you thinking?'

'Well,' said Mossy as he stood up, 'when I came the first time, I was me, in my own clothes, and there wasn't any room for me. When I returned, dressed in these borrowed clothes you invited me in to eat. I was the same person, just the clothes were different. So, you obviously invited the clothes to the meal not me. I fed the clothes!'

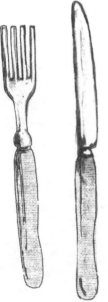

Leib was ashamed. All the men in the room, including the guest, were ashamed.

Leib arranged for the clothes to be cleaned and asked Mossy to take a seat, now dressed in the merchant's best clothes, to eat the *Shabbos* meal in the place of honour.

Even a beggar has his dignity and woe betide those who try to strip him of it.

There was once a *schnorrer* who looked very poor, dressed in rags and with no food or drink. A man was walking past and the *schnorrer* said, 'Please, sir, give some coins to a poor starving beggar.' The man felt pity and put a few coins in the beggar's bowl.

In the evening, he went to a restaurant and there, amazingly, was the beggar eating a great plate of roast duck. The man went up to him and angrily said, 'How come you, a beggar with no money, are here in this expensive restaurant eating DUCK?'

The beggar answered, 'Where do you want me to eat duck if not in a restaurant?'

So many people, chasing so few jobs. The noise was indescribable. Market traders vied with each other to sell their wares. Barrels of pickled cucumbers stood next to barrels of salted herrings. Bagels, hard and chewy, brushed shoulders with black sourdough bread. The rubbish spilled onto the streets as horses and carts jostled their way through to more salubrious areas. Whitechapel was a hubbub of languages; English was in the mix somewhere being bashed around until it fitted the sounds folk were used to. Rooms were let out by the bed. Strangers roomed with strangers. The only thing they had in common was that they were looking for work, any work to earn money to keep them alive or to send back to their families to keep them alive until they could save enough to bring them to this new country. Everyone tried to work as a *cheder* teacher, a teacher of the *alephbeis* to the children of these impoverished immigrants. So many Hebrew teachers and so few jobs. The ones that caught a job knew they were lucky, a bad word away from no job at all and the life of the pedlar. So the lucky few told stories to keep their charges interested and the synagogue boards employing them, stories that helped these children adjust to the new life ahead.

THE PRINCE WHO THOUGHT HE WAS A ROOSTER

The king and queen were worried. Their son, the heir to the kingdom, was a rooster!

Doctors had come, felt the royal brow, held the royal wrist seeking the royal pulse. They had gone away shaking their heads, a triumphant crowing, cock-a-doodle-doo ringing in their ears.

A message went around the kingdom: Anyone who could cure the prince was welcome to try, but woe betide any who failed.

Despite the warning, the queue for the reward snaked around the palace walls, down through the ornate gardens and tailed off in the market streets below. There was an equally long row of spiked heads on pikes.

Eventually the queue got less and less, till it ground to a halt. The king and queen despaired. Their child ran around naked and pecked his food from the floor. He refused to speak except to crow occasionally 'Cock-a doodle-doo!' What were they to do? He was the heir, expected to rule after them …

One day a little old man appeared at the gates.

'I've come to cure the prince,' he declared to the guards, who showed him straight into the throne room. The king and queen sat on their thrones of silver and gold, their faces drawn and grey.

'Have you brought a new medicine to cure our son? We will not allow him to be cut or bled anymore. He pecked the last one to try until they bled instead.'

The little old man bowed before them. 'All I ask is that I am allowed to be with your son alone and that no one questions my methods.'

The royal pair discussed the request. 'You won't hurt him? You won't touch him?'

'What a question! Of course not!'

'Then you have three weeks, before you, too, lose your head.'

The little old man was shown into the room where the prince was contained. It was spacious with little discrete areas. Fine sawdust covered the floor under a layer of rushes. Odd scraps of food were dotted here and there, along with some bowls of water. Feathers

were strewn around, some in clumps, some in bunches, some on their own. The guards inside were relieved to be told they could go and leave the two alone. The prince strutted around the room, naked as the day he was born, lifting his head to crow cock-a doodle-doo, or bending down to peck a crumb of food off the floor.

The little old man studied the prince for a while. Then he took off all his clothes and laid them carefully in a pile, his *arba kanfot* with its *tzitzit*, fringes on top. He followed the prince around the room, copying what he did. After a quick glance to see what the little old man was doing, the prince continued on his path. The little old man followed until the prince was comfortable with him being there, crowing when he crowed, pecking when he pecked, strutting when the prince strutted.

The next morning, the little old man stretched and left his pile of clothes to follow the prince. After a while he went off on his own path around the room. The prince was puzzled and stood still for a bit before joining the little old man.

As he strutted around the room, the little old man began to hum and then sing a wordless song, a *nigun*. Without realising he did so, the prince began to hum the same tune under his breath.

The following day, the little old man started humming his *nigun* straightaway and led the prince around the room. Soon the pair of them were strutting and pecking while singing the *nigun*, only breaking off to crow cock-a doodle-doo! when it struck their fancy.

The next morning, the prince woke up with a cock-a-doodle-doo! Then he began humming the *nigun* as he pecked for his breakfast. The little old man smiled and followed the prince. Suddenly he stopped and spoke to the prince.

'Which way around today, your Highness?'

The prince startled, then said, 'I am a rooster. I don't speak.'

'Ah,' said the little old man, 'but I am a rooster who does speak. Why not? It doesn't stop me being a rooster.'

The prince cocked his head to the side and thought about what the little old man said. He could be a rooster and talk. Why not?

After that the two wandered around the room, pecking, talking, singing and occasionally crowing cock-a-doodle-doo! As the week wound down towards the Sabbath, they talked of this and that and the prince asked questions that the little old man answered, before asking the prince questions himself.

'As it is Shabbos do you think we can eat our food off plates tonight?' asked the little old man.

'But I am a rooster and roosters don't eat off plates,' said the prince.

'I am a rooster who does,' replied the little old man. 'Why not?'

The prince cocked his head to the side and thought. 'Yes,' he declared. 'We are roosters that eat off plates.'

The little old man went to the door and opened it. He told one of the guards to fetch food on plates from now on.

That night they ate their food from plates set on the floor, pecking at it.

'You know what, your Highness, I'm a little old and I find bending down all the time difficult. I am a rooster who uses his hands to eat.'

The prince cocked his head to the side and thought. 'Why not?' he said as he picked up some of the food with his fingers.

During Shabbos the little old man and the prince sang songs and discussed the meaning of Shabbos. The prince wanted to know more and to understand, so the next day the little old man began to scratch the letters of the *alephbeis* in the sawdust. The prince tried making the letters with his feet, then drew them with his fingers. Soon he was able to read and write, though he still strutted and pecked and crowed cock-a-doodle-do!

The little old man watched him and then shivered.

'What's wrong?' asked the prince.

'I am cold,' replied the little old man. 'I need to put some clothes on or I will be ill.'

'Roosters don't wear clothes,' said the prince. 'They have feathers.' And he fluffed out his tail feathers that he had collected from the roosters in the yard and bound into a bunch.

'You're right,' said the little old man, 'but I'm a rooster who does wear clothes. Why not?'

The prince cocked his head to the side and thought.

'If you as a rooster can wear clothes, then I can too!' he declared.

'Ah, but I need to take a bath before I put my clothes back on. The dust baths we take aren't enough,' said the little old man.

'I want a bath, too,' declared the prince.

The little old man went to the door and gave the order for two baths of hot water and fresh clothes for the prince.

Later the pair of them sat, freshly washed and dressed, eating their food from the plates with their fingers.

'A shame to spoil the clothes now we've put them on.'

'We can eat with forks, that would help,' said the prince.

'It would,' agreed the little old man, 'as would sitting at the table.'

'Roosters don't sit at tables,' objected the prince. 'They strut and peck their food in the yard.'

'Well, that's as may be,' said the little old man, 'but I am a rooster who sits and eats at the table. Why not?'

The prince cocked his head to the side and thought. He nodded. The little old man went to the door and soon a table and chairs were in the room.

The pair sat down to their second Shabbos together, dressed and eating at the table.

The following week the king and queen came to visit their son. How astonished they were when they walked in, expecting to see him naked, sporting a bunch of feathers, pecking at the ground. The room was transformed.

Now a carpet lay on the floor, all sawdust and rushes removed. A table laden with books was in the middle and sat on a chair next to it was their son!

They gasped. The queen's eyes filled with tears as she listened to her son explaining the meaning of a passage of the Torah to the little old man, who nodded. The king bit his lip as he saw his child was washed and dressed as befitted a prince.

'Mother, Father,' cried the prince, when he saw them standing in the doorway, 'come in and listen to this tune, isn't it wonderful?' He began to sing the *nigun*.

'Is he cured? Will he stay like this now?' asked the queen in a whisper.

'He will always be a rooster,' answered the little old man. 'But he will be a rooster who behaves like a prince rather than a prince who behaves like a rooster.'

'That's fine by me,' said the king and he grasped the little old man's hand in a strong handshake.

'It's fine by him, too,' said the little old man.

As they grew more affluent, many Jews moved out of the East End. Golders Green in north London is known as a Jewish suburb. Jewish students, living in digs in Golders Green, often had a Sunday job at Grodzinski's the bakers, selling and slicing the favourite rye bread among others. On Shabbat, students would wander from *shtiebl* to *shtiebl* trying them out for size. These were prayer meetings in a house. Someone would decide that they didn't like the way the synagogues were leading the *davening*, praying, and set up their own *minyan*, a quorum of ten men, usually in the front room of their house. Women were allowed but often found themselves in another room or congregating in the corridor between the front door and the kitchen. Sometimes a visiting preacher, a *maggid*, would come and give a talk on the week's *sedra*, portion of the Torah, and then invite questions. There were always questions. This is a story about such a *maggid*.

THE REBBE'S DRIVER

A famous *maggid* travelled from village to town to city preaching and teaching. Wherever he went he was praised for his knowledge. The congregants would crowd round him asking him questions on points of law. More often than not similar questions would come up and the *maggid* would give his answer. Listening to him deliver his sermons and answer his questions was the *maggid*'s long-serving driver.

'*Rebbe*,' said his driver, 'I admire you so much. I can quote your sermons in my sleep. I even know your answers … they ask the same questions time after time.'

The *rebbe* smiled and pulled his beard. 'And?'

'Well, I have a proposition to put to you. We are going to a place we have never been to before. How about I dress as you and you dress as me?'

'Yes?' The *rebbe* was intrigued. 'And then what?'

'Why, I give the sermon and answer the questions. You can see if I have learnt over the years.'

The *rebbe* liked the idea and agreed. They arrived at the next place, the *rebbe* dressed as the driver, the driver dressed as the *rebbe*. They were welcomed by the community with a large *kiddush* after the service. The people all said how much they enjoyed the sermon given by the driver.

Then the questions began. The driver managed to answer all of them. Until there came one from a Torah scholar that hung on a difficult point, a new angle that the driver hadn't heard before. That didn't faze him though.

'What?' exclaimed the driver. 'This is such an easy question, so simple, I can't believe you don't know the answer. You don't need me. Anyone could give you the answer, why not ask my driver over there?' He pointed to the *rebbe*, who smiled and pulled his beard. 'Driver, answer the question!'

RAMSGATE

Ramsgate was the seaside home of Sir Moses Montefiore. He bought a house with 24 acres on East Cliff. Queen Victoria, who had a house next door, liked him so much she had a golden key to his garden and was able to come and visit him and his wife, Judith, whenever she liked. Sir Moses had become more religious after one of his visits to Palestine. He built a synagogue in the grounds, which was opened with a grand public ceremony in 1833.

Sir Moses and Lady Montefiore were the most famous English Jews in Britain at the time. He was Sephardi and she Ashkenazi, a mixed marriage that shocked the Jewish establishment. He was fabulously wealthy, having made it all on the stock exchange when he was a young man. He retired at 40. From then on to the end of his long life – he died aged 100 – he was a philanthropist, doing his best to alleviate suffering wherever he found it, but especially that of Jews across the world.

For this he was knighted and not long after that granted a baronetcy. He and his brother-in-law, Nathan Rothschild, managed to secure a loan for the government to compensate plantation owners, thus enabling the abolition of slavery in the Empire.

He was entertained at the highest tables in the land. At one he famously found himself seated next to a nobleman who was anti-Semitic. This noble waxed lyrical about his trip to Japan, where 'they have neither pigs nor Jews'. Montefiore quickly responded by saying 'in that case, you and I should go there, so it will have a sample of each'.

When he was 89 the local Ramsgate newspaper printed his obituary, which he read and then wrote to the editor, saying, 'Thank

God to have been able to hear of the rumour and to read an account of the same with my own eyes, without using spectacles.'

His house has been demolished but the synagogue and mausoleum where he and his wife are buried are able to be visited on request.

This Sephardi tale explores the same theme of loving kindness that the Montefiores pursued all their long lives.

THE GOLDEN TREE

Ilana loved plants. Succulents, hairy, flat-leaved, narrow-tipped, bushy, creeping – anything really as long as it was green. That's not quite true, most of all, Ilana loved trees. She had made studying them, dendrology, her life's work. She was happy among trees. Whisper it quietly, but she hugged them … a lot. She couldn't imagine a life without a tree in it. That was why she was so surprised to get a text from the *shadchan*, the matchmaker. Marriage hadn't encroached on her horizon. It wasn't something she had planned on. Still, she was intrigued enough to agree to go on a date. After all, the *shadchan* had texted; whoever it was had to do what Ilana liked best.

Rotem was fed up. His father insisted that he had to marry. He was the heir to a large fortune and his father didn't want it to be dissipated in loose living. He thought if Rotem married he would settle down and some of the excess behaviour might cease. To stop his father going on and on, Rotem agreed to meet the four women the *shadchan* had selected. Trying to make the dates interesting for him, the *shadchan* had arranged for each girl to take Rotem out rather than the other way round.

Zahavah loved sailing. She had taken control of the boat as soon as they boarded. She was determined to put Rotem in his place and show what she could do best. Rotem enjoyed the buzz of sailing, the wind in his hair, the speed over the water. He loved the date. He wasn't that keen on Zahavah, she was too intent on showing him how much better than him she was. He'd been sailing since he was a boy. He'd won cups!

Miri took him rock climbing. At one point Rotem dangled over a shelf, connected by a camming device and carabiners attached to his harness. He loved the rush of adrenaline. He could do that again, but not necessarily with Miri. She had been abrupt and spoke little except to tell him where to put his feet or which was the better grip. Rotem grimaced at the thought of a life being told what to do.

Next was Ariela who took him surfing. He'd fallen off many times, but when he caught the wave, it was like nothing else in the world. Ariela was nice, pleasant. He could get used to her.

Ilana took him for a walk in the wood. At first Rotem was sceptical; what was so great about walking in the woods? But despite his antipathy, he began to feel calm. He relaxed and started joking with Ilana. He found she matched him, witticism for witticism. Peace stole over him. Ilana loved the fact he accepted her as she was. One date led to another.

Surprising himself, Rotem told his father that he'd found his bride. His father was overjoyed. The wedding celebrations were huge and lavish. Ilana was a bit taken aback. She had never worried about money, but neither had she seen it being used so extravagantly. She hoped Rotem didn't expect them to live like that after the wedding.

One night after they had returned from honeymoon, Ilana had a dream. There was a tree, not unusual in itself, but this was a golden tree. It had roots reaching down into the earth and a strong trunk stretching up with branches spiralling off. Leaves of gold tinkled and globes of golden fruit hung together.

It was such a strong dream that Ilana knew she had to find the golden tree. As luck would have it, she'd been offered the opportunity of going on a field trip to classify new species of trees. Her golden tree might be among them.

Rotem blew up. He couldn't believe Ilana would bail on him this early in their marriage. How long would she be away? A year? At the least? He demanded she choose … him … or trees. Did she want to save her marriage? Or were the trees more important? He gave her an ultimatum – stay or leave!

Ilana felt she had no choice. What do you think? You're right, she left.

Rotem threw himself into partying hard. He went sailing with Zahavah, rock climbing with Miri and surfing with Ariela. Somehow there was something missing. He couldn't work out what it was.

One night he had a dream. He dreamt of a golden tree whose roots reached far down into the earth. Its trunk was solid and straight. Its

branches spiralled up and outwards. It was covered in golden leaves and golden globes of fruit hung down. Dreaming, Rotem felt a sense of peace. Awakening, he still felt it.

He consulted his rabbi who interpreted dreams. 'What is the meaning of this dream, Rabbi?'

The rabbi didn't hesitate. 'Find the golden tree and you will find true love.'

Still puzzled but determined, Rotem set off with just a rucksack on his back. He sailed here and there. He walked far and further. He climbed hill and mountain until his shoes wore out and the skin on his feet yellowed and hardened. His clothes grew ragged and his beard and hair grew long and unkempt. And on he searched.

One day he followed a winding path through a forest until he came to a clearing with water ahead. The water bubbled and steamed. Salt pans lay like stepping stones in the roiling water. Across the water, through the steam trails, he glimpsed a gleam of gold. His heart beat faster. He was near his journey's end, he knew it. With no thought for safety, he plunged straight across the boiling salt pans. Each step he took burned off a layer of horned skin. By the time he reached the other side his feet were pink and soft as a baby's. Rotem fell on his knees.

In front of him was a golden tree, roots reaching down into the earth, trunk solid and straight, branches spiralling upwards. And the leaves, the golden leaves tinkled together sounding like Ilana's voice. The golden globes of fruit reflected her face.

Tears fell fast and furious, streaming down his cheeks as he realised what he had done. Ilana was his heart's peace. He knew that with a certainty he hadn't before. He felt reborn. Rotem broke off a branch of the golden tree with its leaves and fruit intact. He packed it carefully into his rucksack. By the time he was ready to return the water had cooled and he was able to cross without injury.

Using his sources, Rotem soon found where Ilana was. He came upon her in a secluded part of the Indian rainforest, classifying plants. He watched her, in her element. For the first time he realised what he had asked her to give up to remain with him.

Ilana started when she saw a strange man approach her. His skin was leathered and lined, his hair and beard greyed. He was thin, too thin. Then he pulled out the branch of the golden tree. In the tinkling of its leaves she heard Rotem's voice, his face in the reflection of its golden globes of fruit. She heard him beg her for forgiveness.

They talked long into the night while the insects buzzed around them. The pull of the golden tree was strong in both, they were like puzzle pieces that slotted together. Rotem felt his heart's peace. Now they were talking they could agree Ilana's career was important to her. Rotem would do all he could to support her. They established the Golden Tree Nursery for exotic plants, saving and propagating rare plants wherever they were found, relocating those threatened by extinction when their environment was compromised.

And not long after they were in need of a different kind of nursery.

OXFORD

Jews had arrived in Oxfordshire as early as 1080 when a man named Manasses is mentioned in the Domesday Book as living in the village of Bletchtingdon. The Jews, from Rouen, were literate and numerate and although banned from the guilds, were the bankers and money lenders to the barons and the Crown, paying a high tax for the privilege.

By 1141 the Jews of Oxford were being oppressed by both King Stephen and Queen Matilda in their civil war. Both needed money at the same time for their separate armies and when the Jews couldn't pay, the Crown had Aaron ben Isaac's house burned down. Most of the Jews lived south of Carfax in St Aldgate's, which became known as Great Jewry Street. A synagogue was built and a *mikveh*, ritual bath, the remnants of which can still be seen.

Ironically the first college to be founded in Oxford, Merton College, was originally Jacob of London's property, Bek's Hall. As an old, infirm man, he sold the property to Bishop Walter de Merton in 1264. The contract is in Latin and Hebrew and is the oldest collegiate document to survive. It is ironic because Jews were barred from attending the University until 1856 and holding a fellowship until 1871. Nowadays Oxford is one of the most vibrant Jewish communities with all sides of Judaism living and worshipping if not together then in the same building and sharing *kiddush* afterwards. How can this be?

A couple went to a rabbi to mediate their upcoming divorce. The rabbi listened to the man and said, 'You're right.' He then listened to the woman and said, 'You're right.' His student, who had been following the arguments on both sides, said to him, 'Rabbi, they can't both be right!' The rabbi turned to him and said, 'You're also right!'

Rabbi Berechiah the Punctuator, the Jewish Aesop, lived in Oxford in the late twelfth century. His book *Mishle Shualim* (Fox Fables) is a Hebrew version of *Aesop's Fables* with a Jewish twist as well as his own created fables. He frequently changed the animal or setting, or added in a Biblical reference. He often wrote in rhymed prose with a firm moral at the end.

Here is one of his tales.

Ewe, Goat and Shepherd

A ewe, ready to drop her lamb, was in the farmyard. Outside the farmyard, in a field by a hedge, was a nanny goat. The shepherd watched and waited for the ewe to give birth. He was worried she would reject her young. When he saw she had delivered and indeed had rejected her lamb, he took it from her and brought it to the goat. The nanny goat suckled the lamb, who grew big. She looked after it and cared for it as if it was hers. When the lamb was weaned, the goat said, 'Look to your ways. Return to your birthplace and do great deeds. Your mother was a ewe, your father a ram. I may have brought you up and looked after you and cared for you, but your parents will be happy to see you as you are now, returned to your people.'

The sheep answered, 'No, you are my mother, for you have loved me and looked after me. I won't call the ewe my mother because she pushed me far away from her home and would see me no more. I have no desire to see her.'

Give ear to the parable and listen: He who treats you well and cares for you, count him as a relation. On the other hand, he who doesn't want to know you even though you are related, count him nothing in a crowd. That kind of person you don't want to be bothered with. He troubles his kin and is cruel. He stores up trouble for himself if he says: 'None may love me except he be related to me for that gives me honour amongst the dwellers of the world: 'tis a brother who is born for time of trouble.'

෴

A mother bought her son two new ties, one blue, one green. The son wanted to wear one to his interview in Oxford the next day. He couldn't decide which to wear and asked his mother.

'Choose the one that matches your suit best,' replied his mother.

He came down dressed with the blue tie.

His mother took one look at him.

'You didn't like the green one?'

NORWICH

A Jew, Isaac, is mentioned in the Domesday Book as living in Norwich. Many of the Jews were moneylenders and lived under the protection of the king, settling below the castle in what is now White Lion Street. The medieval synagogue was built where the Lamb Inn now stands. The Jews were French speaking and kept themselves to themselves.

When a Jew is dying there are rituals to be gone through, the final confession, the ritual blessing of the children like the patriarchs of old, laying hands on their heads.

Jurnet's House

Jurnet, the richest man in Norwich, lay dying. He had tried to live his life full of *mitzvot (*good deeds), *tzedaka* (charity) and *tzedek* (justice). He had lent money so that churches, cathedrals and castles could be built, including Norwich Cathedral. Now, he lay in his house in King Street, just below the castle. He called his three sons to him.

'My sons,' he quavered, 'I have lived a long life. I hope and pray you will live a life in peace with one another. I have never sworn in anger. Please remember that quarrelling leads to swearing and so try not to quarrel. Love God, as your mother and I taught you, all the days of your life so your days may be lengthened.* Live in this house and take care of my beautiful herb garden. Guard it from

---

* Slight misquote from the Ten Commandments, sedra Yitro, Exodus.

thieves in the night. Bless you as Jacob blessed his sons and the sons of Joseph.'

Not long after, the old man died. The sons buried him, as was the custom, the same day on the other side of the River Wensum. During the mourning period, *shiva*, the sons remembered their father's wishes and took turns to stand guard over the herb garden. The eldest went first, as was his right and his duty.

Whilst he was on watch an old man appeared before him out of the mist.

'Who are you?' he challenged.

'I am Elijah the Prophet and I have come to reward you for following your father's wishes.'

The eldest son was taken aback. 'What kind of reward?'

'You have a choice of three,' answered Elijah. 'Choose wisely or they may be taken back.'

'What are these three choices then? Tell me for I am ready to hear them.'

'You can have great wealth, great knowledge or marry a good wife,' said Elijah.

The eldest son didn't rush into a decision. He thought them over carefully. If he was rich, he could buy any book he wanted or the services of a scholar. Everyone in the community would be clamouring to accept him as a son-in-law. He could have his pick of the young women for his wife. His choice was made for him.

'I will take great wealth,' he said.

Elijah pressed a coin into his hand. 'Keep hold of this, for your good fortune relies on it.'

The eldest son curled his fingers over the coin and raised his head to thank the old man, only to find he had disappeared. He

went back into the house at the end of his watch but didn't say anything to his brothers.

The following night it was the second son's turn. He too was approached by Elijah and offered a reward for following his father's wishes. What would he choose? Wealth, knowledge or a good wife? He thought long and hard. He had always wanted to travel and while great wealth would help him on his way, he wouldn't be able to get to know the people and to give them something of himself. He prided himself on his learning. A wife wasn't someone he was interested in, not at the moment. His choice was made.

'Great knowledge please,' he said.

Elijah handed him a book. 'Look after this with great care. You can find all the knowledge in the world and out of it, here.'

The second son handled the book as if it were made of glass. 'Thank you,' he said, but Elijah had disappeared.

The next night it was the third son's turn. He was astonished when Elijah appeared in front of him. His brothers had not mentioned their nights to him at all except to say they were uneventful.

'What is your choice?' asked Elijah after giving him the same options.

'A good wife, please,' said the third son with no hesitation. He knew he had a third of his father's wealth and a third of the house. He knew he was no scholar.

'After the *shiva* is over, you and I will go off to London. Tell your brothers you will be away for a while.'

Five days later Elijah joined the third son and they left the castle surrounds and set off due south. His brothers had paid him no mind and asked no questions. They were full of their own plans.

After walking steadily for the best part of a day, the pair came to an inn. The innkeeper and his wife looked them up and down, dusty as they were, before offering them a bed over the stables. Elijah took it. The innkeeper's daughter showed them the way. She had a sharp pointed face and indicated where they were to sleep rather than talk to them.

That night Elijah was woken by the talking of the animals below them. He, like King Solomon, could understand the language of animals.

'I hope Elijah knows what he's doing, bringing the lad here,' said the donkey. 'The daughter doesn't fall far from her tree.'

'True, true,' said the horse. 'The hay they've given me is old and stale and the water has so many flies in it.'

Elijah smiled to himself as he fell asleep.

The two travellers moved on in the morning, walking forever southwards. Eventually they came to another inn, with two rosy innkeepers. Their daughter chatted merrily as she showed them to their preferred bed in the stables.

That night Elijah woke again to hear the chat of the animals.

'This girl is as flighty as her parents are spendthrifts,' came the report.

In the morning Elijah and the young man walked on, turning west towards London. Evening overcame them well before they reached the capital and they stopped for the night at an inn on the outskirts. They ate well, listening to the tales of the innkeeper and adding a few of their own. The third son was taken by the daughter, who seemed to do all her chores with a smile on her face.

Insisting on a bed in the stables, Elijah and the third son prepared for sleep, saying their prayers. The daughter of the house brought them a jug of cool water and then saw to the animals before she left. Their mattresses were stuffed with sweet-smelling hay.

The chat that night was quiet, the animals were eating and drinking, before they too fell asleep.

In the morning Elijah nudged the third son. 'This is the one, this is your good wife.'

The third son needed no nudging. He saw for himself as he ate the fresh crusty bread, baked that morning. He talked to the girl and then he talked to the innkeeper and his wife. They came to an arrangement. The girl would follow him in a few weeks, giving him time to prepare for a wedding. Elijah and the third son turned for home.

When they arrived, they found the eldest son had moved out. He had bought new premises down the street and was already courting the daughter of the rabbi. The second son had packed and caught a boat to the Continent. He was going to lecture in Amsterdam, before travelling further inland.

The third son got the house and garden ready for his bride. She came with her parents and they were married soon after. They lived happily in Jurnet's house, filling it with love, laughter and children. The garden was well tended. As it was a herb garden, the wife decided to make up her own remedies for ills. These proved very popular in the town. She often took them to the synagogue in White Lion Street to be available for any who needed. Life was good.

The eldest son and his wife had bought an estate as business had prospered. They had two children who were brought up by the servants. One day an old beggar appeared at the gates of the mansion and was turned away. Somehow, he slipped in and walked up the long drive to the house. At the front door he was again turned away and threatened with the dogs. He demanded to see the master of the house.

Eventually the old man was allowed into the library. The eldest son was aghast when he realised who the old man was. Elijah was not happy.

'Great wealth was given to you to do great things with it. To help the poor, to feed the widows and orphans, to provide education for all. You have kept it for yourself. You do not deserve it. Give me back the coin.'

Despite all the blustering and excuses he could make, the eldest son had to return the coin. Elijah left without another word. Immediately, all the eldest son's businesses began to fail. The estate was sold, the servants let go. There was only one place the eldest son, his wife and his two children could go to before they too ended in the poorhouse.

The second son enjoyed his life on the Continent. His fame spread far and wide, he was welcomed and feted wherever he went. People turned to him for his knowledge rivalled any of the fabled heads of *yeshivot*, houses of study of the Torah. If there was a particularly abstruse point, he was called upon. He loved displaying his wisdom in crowded rooms full of students.

One day an old man appeared at one of his lectures. The old man listened and watched carefully and then asked a question of his own. The second son dismissed the question and the questioner as foolish. Elijah was incensed.

'I gave you the book to spread knowledge in the world. To enable others to sharpen their wits, to raise themselves above their calling by studying, to enable wisdom to be passed on. What are you doing by demeaning them and their questions? You are setting yourself up as the only arbiter of knowledge. This was not what the book was for. Give it back.'

No matter how the scholar argued, Elijah was intransigent. The book was handed over. It wasn't long after that the scholar found that without the book, he couldn't remember a thing. His circuit of lectures was cancelled. There was only one place he could go.

In Jurnet's house, his son Isaac took pleasure in his wife's management of the house and especially the herb garden. There was room at his table for visitors and friends whenever they came. Elijah had smiled and gone away without announcing his presence. Even the eldest brother, wife and children had been found enough space for them to live in and they were soon joined by the second son. All three brothers lived the rest of their lives in their father's house, content with what they had.

Isaac is noted as still living there in 1197.

Hull

Wherever Jews settle usually three things follow in quick succession: a synagogue or room in a house used for prayers, with a room for studying, *cheder* (but be careful, in slang Yiddish asking if you've been to *cheder* means have you been to prison); a ritual bath, *mikveh*, usually attached to a local baths, used by the men every Friday afternoon and before the festivals and often used by the women only at night; and a cemetery that serves the wider community, sometimes for hundreds of miles around.

Once the land has been bought for burial, the community walks the bounds seven times saying psalms and prayers. A Jewish prayer book that can no longer be used is then buried in the grounds. This is when the book is very old and has pages missing or torn, words worn away. Torah scrolls and prayer books that have the name of God written in them cannot be burned or shredded. They have to be treated with the same respect as if they were whole and usable. They are usually collected and buried in the same grave as a body, if possible.

Stories about death, dying and the dead are common to all Jewish communities, often with a leavening of humour.

Not far from his business in Market Square, a jeweller lay dying in his house in Hull. His family gathered around him.

'Ruth, are you here?' quavered the old man.

'I'm here, Dad,' his eldest daughter answered with a catch in her voice.

'Shimon, are you here?'

'Yes, Dad, I'm here.'

'Ben, Benjamin, you here, too?'

His younger son sobbed, 'Yes, Dad.'

'Esther, you?'

'Of course, Dad, where else would we be?'

'Then who is looking after the shop?'

The practice is to bury the body within three days but preferably on the day of death and never on the Sabbath, which starts just before sunset on Friday and lasts until an hour after sunset on Saturday. All Jews are buried in the simplest box, without ornament, for death makes us all the same. In Hull, in the Hessle Street cemetery, now grassed over, there was a notable burial, not for how rich or well-known the person was, nor how famous he was for studying the Torah. No, this was the burial of the jeweller, Abraham Samuel.

CLOCKING OFF

It was two o'clock on a Friday morning when Abraham Samuel breathed his last. His friends, who had gathered round him, discussed what they should do. 'He's Jewish, he should be buried as a Jew,' insisted one.

'But where do Jews get buried? Here in Scarborough?' asked another.

'I don't think so,' said the first. 'Wasn't Abraham the only Jew hereabouts?'

'Then we'll have to get him to Hull. I know there's a Jewish cemetery there,' said a third.

'How are we going to do that then? I mean, we can't just put him on the coach as he is and send him there, can we?'

They looked at each other and formed a plan.

By 6.30a.m. they had arrived at the coaching inn in Scarborough with a long wooden box. They booked a ticket for the box all the way to Hull. The label was filled out carefully: 'One long case clock to be delivered to the Jewish community cemetery house in Hessle Street, Hull. Fragile, handle with care.'

The clock was accepted and placed on the 7 a.m. coach to Hull.

Forty miles and hours later the horses drew in to the Hull coach station and the clock was unloaded. It was reloaded onto a delivery cart and sent on its way to the Jewish cemetery.

There was consternation when the clock arrived at the *ohel*. The members of the *Chevra Kadisha*, the Holy Brotherhood that take care of the dead, weren't expecting a timepiece and opened the box gingerly to find the corpse of Abraham Samuel. His friends had enclosed a letter explaining all.

The *Chevra Kadisha* went into overdrive. They called the gravediggers in and had the grave dug as fast as possible. While that was going on, they hurried around gathering a *minyan*, to say the prayers over the body when it would be buried. They washed the body and dressed it in its white shroud. Then they replaced the body in the long case clock box and lowered him into the newly dug grave.

Ten men said *kaddish*, the prayer for the dead, over his grave as the July afternoon deepened. Abraham Samuel was sent to his rest just before the Sabbath started at sunset. Clocked off, just in time.

LEEDS

Leeds, unlike other cities, had no established Sephardi community. The majority of immigrants were working-class Ashkenazi. By 1877 there were about 500 Jewish families and this rose steeply to 25,000 by 1907. Many people came to Leeds because their relatives or friends had already settled there, as the city became the tailoring centre of the Empire. Owners of tailoring workshops sent for fellow tailors from their home towns. Others came because they knew someone who would give them a job in a tailoring factory. They settled in the Leylands area of Leeds, which has now been redeveloped. But the schools around these streets were Jewish, the shops were Jewish. Non-Jewish neighbours often came in on a Saturday to light the fire for observant Jews, who were not allowed to light a flame on the Sabbath. As the Jews could not ask the neighbours to light the fire for themselves alone, the neighbours often stayed and shared a biscuit and a cup of tea and, of course, a story or two.

This story is based upon a well-known Yiddish nursery song.

Hob Ikh Mir a Mantl (I Had a Little Overcoat)

In a small squashed house in Lovell Street, Leylands, Leeds lived a boy, his mother and his grandfather. They all lived together happily. His grandfather, *zayde*, was a tailor. All day he sat in the old way, *fis* on a *fis*, foot upon foot, to sew the clothes. His mother worked in a textile mill. Shmuelik was looked after by one of the neighbours for a small charge.

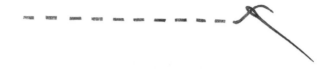

One day his mother brought home a small bolt of beautiful cloth.

'*Tati*, look what I got today from the mill. Mr Freidman let me have it at lower than cost price. I thought Shmuelik would look wonderful in this, *keynahora*. What do you think?'

Her father fingered the material, feeling the softness and quality within the weave. '*Takke*, it's a lovely piece, but there's not much of it. I'll have a think and see what I can do.'

All night he thought and moved his pattern pieces around. Finally, as he sat, *fis* on a *fis*, he cut and he sewed.

In the morning Shmuelik came downstairs for breakfast to find a wonderful new coat on his chair. 'Thank you, *Zayde*,' he said as he tried it on. He ran straight off to school to show all his friends. 'Look at the cut, the style. Isn't it fine?' Everyone agreed it was indeed lovely.

Shmuelik wore the coat every day, even in the heat of summer. Mind, up in Leeds the wind often swirled around the huddled terraces of Leylands. Even so he was upset when the coat did as coats do and became a little threadbare here and a little shiny there.

He went to his mother, who had come home from working in the mill. 'Mum, I love this coat, but it's too small. Is there anything you can do?'

His mother looked at the coat and then at her son. 'Why don't you go upstairs and ask *Zayde*? I'm sure he'll help you.'

So Shmuelik trudged up the stairs wearing his coat. His grandfather looked up from the stool where he sat, *fis* on a *fis*. 'Shmuelik, *zieskeit*, why such a long face?'

'*Zayde*, I love this coat but it's too small and worn out. Can you do anything?'

His *zayde* patted Shmuelik on the cheek. 'I'll have a think. You go off to bed.'

Shmuelik went to bed and his *zayde* had a think. He thought and then, *fis* on a *fis*, cut off the bad bits and sewed together the good bits. In the morning Shmuelik came down to find a jacket waiting for him.

'Oh, how wonderful it is, my favourite material! Thank you, *Zayde*.' He gave his *zayde* a kiss and off he went to the Gower Street school.

'Look at the cut, the style. Isn't it fine?' he asked his friends. They all agreed it was indeed lovely.

Shmuelik wore the jacket every day with either of his two pairs of trousers. He wore it to school, he wore it to *cheder*, he wore it to *shul* in Belgrave Street.

Eventually though, Shmuelik did what boys do and grew. The jacket became a little threadbare here and a little shiny there. One day he went home to his mother, who had come back from work. 'Mum, I love this jacket but it's too small and worn out. Is there anything you can do?'

His mother, her hands inside the chicken she was kashering for Shabbos, pulling out the *pupikl* and *kishke*, looked at the jacket and then at her son. 'Why don't you go upstairs and ask *Zayde*? I'm sure he'll help you.'

Shmuelik climbed the stairs and knocked on his *zayde*'s door. His grandfather looked up from the chair where he sat in the window, saying, 'Such a long face should never be seen, it can curdle the cream.'

'*Zayde*,' said Shmuelik, 'I love my jacket but it is too small. Can you do anything?'

'I'll have a think. See you in the morning,' said his *zayde* as he felt the cloth.

Well, he thought and then, *fis* on a *fis*, he cut off the bad bits and sewed together the good bits.

In the morning Shmuelik came down to find a waistcoat waiting for him. 'Oh *Zayde*, it's wonderful!' He kissed his *zayde* and went off to school. 'Look at the cut, the style. Isn't it fine?' he asked his friends. They all agreed it was wonderful.

Shmuelik wore the waistcoat at his interview as an apprentice presser. He wore the waistcoat all day every day. He wanted to wear it on his *bar mitzvah*, but waistcoats and growing boys don't always match. He came home one day with the back all ripped. His mother looked up from the grinder attached to the kitchen table where she was making *kreplach* from the left-over meat. 'Go and ask your *zayde*,' she said before he could ask.

Shmuelik went upstairs to his grandfather's room. He knocked and went in. His grandfather was sitting in his chair with his eyes closed, resting. '*Zayde*?' asked Shmuelik quietly, '*Zayde*?' His grandfather opened an eye. He took in the split waistcoat and Shmuelik's shame-filled but beseeching face. 'Leave it on the side, boy. I'll have a think.'

Well, Shmuelik's *zayde* thought. He stayed in his chair, cut off all the bad bits and sewed together the good bits.

In the morning Shmuelik came down to find a tie made out of his favourite material. 'Oh, *Zayde*, thank you. It's wonderful,' he said as he tied the tie round his neck. 'I'll be the envy of all the apprentices.' And he ran off to find his friends.

'Look at this tie, the cut, the style. Isn't it fine?' His friends agreed that it was indeed lovely.

Shmuelik wore the tie as often as he could. He wore it on his first date with a girl. It was his lucky tie. But ties do as ties do and it frayed a bit here and wore a bit there.

It was a sad day when he went home to find his mother peering over her glasses at the mending she was doing. 'Mum, my lucky tie …' His mother didn't say anything but pointed up the stairs. To be fair she had a mouthful of pins.

Shmuelik took the stairs two at a time. He tapped softly on his *zayde*'s door.

'Come in, a person could catch a cold the time you are standing there with the door open,' said his *zayde* with a quaver in his voice. He was sat in his armchair by the window. His eyes closed against the fading warmth of the sun.

'*Zayde?*'

Shmuelik held out his tie. His grandfather opened one eye. He opened the other. 'Again?'

Shmuelik nodded. His *zayde* nodded. 'I'll have a think,' he said before he shut his eyes. Shmuelik crept out of the room, shutting the door quietly behind him.

His *zayde* thought and then he cut off the bad bits and sewed together the good bits. In the morning Shmuelik came down to find waiting for him ... a button, covered in the beautiful cloth. He picked it up and sewed it on his jacket. He ran up the stairs to wake his grandfather. 'Thank you, *Zayde*. Thank you.'

He ran off to work and showed all his friends as he took his jacket off, changing into his apron. 'Look at this, isn't it fine?' They all agreed it was wonderful.

But Shmuelik's sewing wasn't as good as his mother's. His sewing wasn't as good as his grandfather's. The button came loose and soon fell off without him noticing. When he did, he came home embarrassed. His mother shook her head and he went upstairs to his *zayde*.

'*Zayde?*'

His *zayde* was lying down on his bed, a blanket covering his frail limbs. He opened one eye. '*Nu?* Again?'

Shmuelik nodded.

His *zayde* sighed.

'Even I can't make something out of nothing.'

Shmuelik sighed. It seemed the end of that beautiful material. Until his grandfather, having thought, opened the other eye. Shmuelik's heart lifted.

'Yes?'

'Well ...' said his *zayde*, 'what I have made is ...'

'Yes?' said Shmuelik eagerly.

'Is this story especially for you out of the nothing you have brought me.'

And so it was, and so it is, and so it will always be.

1. *Hob ikh mir a mantl fun fartsaytikn tukh*
Tra-la-la … Iz in im nishto keyn gantsner dukh
Tra-la-la … Darum, hob ikh zikh batrakht Un fun dem mantl a rekl
gemakht. Tra-la-la …
Fun dem mantl a rekl gemakht
2. *Hob ikh mir a rekl … fun dem rekl a vestl gemakht*
3. *Vestl … shnipsl*
4. *shnipsl … knepl*
5. *knepl … gornitl*
6. *gornit … dos lidele.*

1. I had a little overcoat, as old as can be
Tra-la-la … What I'd ever do with it, I just couldn't see
Tra-la-la … So I thought for a while and from that overcoat I made
a little jacket. Tra-la-la …
2. From the jacket … I made a waistcoat
3. Waistcoat … tie
4. Tie … button
5. Button … nothing
6. Nothing … this song.

Hob ikh mir a mant-tl fun far - tzay - ti - kn tukh, Tra – la-la – la-la - la-la - la - la - la - la.

Iz in im nish-to keyn gan - tse-nerdukh, Tra-la-la - la - la - la-la - la - la - la-la-la. Da – rum

hob ikh zikh ba-trakht un fundem man - tl a re – kl ge-makht Tra - la-la - la-la - la - la.

Tra – la-la – la-la - la - la. Un fun dem man - tl a re – kl ge-makht.

Jews didn't have surnames as such. They had a patronymic in Hebrew, *ben* (son of) e.g. ben Aaron, or *ovitch* in Russian, for example, Aaronovitch. A person could have three distinct names that were theirs: the Hebrew name they were given at birth, the secular name and the name they were given at immigration control. Sometimes they couldn't understand what was being asked. 'What is your name?' got the common reply '*Ikh bin* Dov, Reuben's *zohn*' (I am Dov, Reuben's son) and they were written down forever as Dov Rubenstein. Sometimes a newly married woman with the same name as her mother-in-law would have to change her first name out of respect, so everyone would know which Bluma was which. Often though they took the name of their occupation, like the English Cooper, or Smith or Tailor. In Leeds there were many people coming to produce the cloth and suits that the city was becoming famous for. Among them were the Shneiders or Hyatts; both tailors, one in Yiddish one in Hebrew.

As so many Jews were working for the tailoring industry in Leeds, they became greatly involved in the labour movement. They were the backbone of the Jewish Tailors' Machinists' and Pressers'

Union and had a strong influence on the Jewish community as a whole. They had a club that seemed to represent all of Leeds Jewry to the outside world.

How the Moon Got Her Garment

Do you know why they invented Lycra? They were trying to copy the material that Yankel made for the moon. You don't know the story? How the moon was fed up with the fact that her clothes didn't fit the whole month. Sometimes they fell off her, sometimes they were too tight. She wanted to wear a garment that fitted her all month round. She moaned; she complained to the sun, who loved the moon very much. 'You blaze so hot all day, you don't need clothes, but I light the night and sometimes it is very cold. I need something to wear, something that will grow when I grow and shrink when I shrink.'

The sun decided that the moon was right. She needed a garment to wear when it was cold. He launched a competition among the best designers in the world:

Create a garment for the moon that will change as she changes.

He offered a great prize, more wealth than any could dream of, for he loved the moon very much and he wanted her to be happy.

Well, the designers fell over themselves to create the best for the sun, sorry, the moon. The sun liked all the designs but there was one huge flaw … the designers hadn't specified a material.

'Don't worry,' they told the sun, who did indeed worry, 'our team of tailors will fix this. They know all the weavers. Give us a year.' The designers walked off in the certain knowledge that the tailors would once again pull their logs out of the fire.

The tailors gathered in their union hall. The discussion was loud and voluble. Arguments broke out in separate groups. Soon no one could be heard under a hundred decibels.

'There is no such material!' shouted one faction.

'We know,' shouted another, 'but who will tell the designers?'

'Whoever heard of such a thing?' shouted yet another.

'I have,' said a quiet voice. No one listened. No one heard.

'I have,' said the owner of the voice a bit louder. A few people around heard and stopped shouting.

'I have,' said the tailor once more.

'Shah! Shah!' came the cry, shushing the other tailors. 'He says he has.'

'He has what?'

'I have heard of such a material. My father told me once of a country far away whose queen was always married in the same heirloom dress that fitted no matter the size of the queen.'

'*Bubbemeises*! Fairy tales!' came the cry. 'We expect nothing less from Yankel. He lives with his head in the air.'

'But,' said a wiser head, 'we have nothing to lose if Yankel goes to find this material and brings it back. If he manages it, we are the winners. If he doesn't, well we can always say, "It was Yankel! So what did you expect?"'

There were nods at this wise man. Who knew if Yankel would succeed? Who knew if Yankel could succeed? But no one else had any idea what to do. Yankel's idea was half-baked but it was better than no bread at all.

The tailors pooled their pennies and gave all they could afford to Yankel. They hoped the money would last as long as he needed but there was no guarantee. They made sure he had enough food to last a couple of days. He started off on his journey with the blessing for travel ringing in his ears.

Yankel set off with a song in his heart and strong boots on his feet. He knew he had to travel a long way to find the country where the queen with the wonderful garment lived. He walked over hills, he walked down valleys, he crossed rivers. Wherever he walked he asked about the country that had a magical garment that fitted no matter the size of the queen.

Everyone he spoke to laughed at him. *Bubbemeises*! Fairy tales! There was no such country, no such queen, no such material. Yankel shook his head and travelled on. He walked up hills, he walked down valleys, he crossed rivers. Everywhere he went he asked about the queen with the magical garment. His time was running out. He was beginning to lose hope. His feet slogged the miles, slower and slower.

Until one day, as he was on a ferry crossing one more river, an old man cackled.

'Ah, the magical garment of the queen. Why everyone knows about that.'

'What?' cried Yankel. 'Where?'

'Why in the city over the hills, across this river.'

Yankel lifted his eyes up and blessed the old man.

He jumped off the ferry and stretched his legs to get there as fast as possible. His heart lifted in hope. Over one more hill!

There was the city in all its glory, but it was a city with no joy, no singing, no dancing, no laughter.

'What's the matter?' Yankel asked one of the people hurrying away from the market.

'It's the princess. She is supposed to get married at the end of the month, but the queen has forbidden her to marry. She's stopped visitors to the palace, too. We don't know what's gone wrong.'

Yankel shook his head. His heart dropped. 'Can no one see the queen?' he asked.

'No one,' came the answer, 'except tailors or seamstresses.'

'What did you say? Tailors or seamstresses? Why that's me. I'm them. Tailors or seamstresses. Tailors. Tailor. That's me. I'm a tailor.' He laughed. 'I'm a tailor, I'm a tailor. I can see the queen.' He danced on the spot.

Not long after Yankel was in a private audience with the queen.

She was an elegant, compact woman, who looked tired and wan.

'I am taking you into my confidence, please don't repeat anything I say outside of these walls. The consequences are dire … for you.'

Yankel promised. He didn't want to find out what the consequences would be.

'My family has an heirloom. A robe that every princess or queen has worn on their wedding day. It is said whoever marries without it, the marriage is doomed to failure. Usually the robe alters to fit the shape of the woman wearing it, but there is so little left …' The queen broke off. She swallowed. 'The material has been disappearing thread by thread for a long time. I can't let my daughter get married. I'm breaking her heart, but I daren't risk it. Here!' She snapped her fingers. A page entered with a tray bearing shimmering stuff.

Yankel touched it gently. He had never seen such wonderful material. This was the fabled fabric. His quest was at an end. All he had to do was ask for some of it to take back to make the garment for the moon. As he watched, a loose thread waved in the air and slowly disappeared.

'You see what is happening, what has been happening for so long? The way to weave new threads has been lost over the years. There was enough to make my robe, but now the threads are too few for my daughter. Can you help?'

Yankel's heart dropped. He didn't know what to do. He asked for a room on his own and time to examine the material closely.

The queen gave him what he asked for. He spent all day, thinking, touching. He had to be careful for the slightest movement caused another thread to break free and disappear. But for all his thinking he found no solution. He despaired. He was lost. His quest had ended in failure, he couldn't help the queen and her daughter either. He prayed for help, for guidance.

Without him noticing, the room had grown dark. Sunset had passed. The moon had risen. He had no candle to see by. He picked up the material and held it up to the only light, moonlight, streaming through the window.

The silver light touched the stuff. To Yankel's astonishment, the light caught a flowing thread and spun more. He turned the stuff around in the moonlight. Every time the moonlight hit, more threads grew and as he turned, they wove themselves into the material. The material grew under his fingers, soft, shimmering, pliable.

Yankel thanked God. He praised the moon. He laughed. He danced. As he danced the material grew and stretched in the moonlight. Yankel wrapped it round himself, laughing all the while.

By the time the moon had set the material had doubled, tripled in size. Yankel fell asleep with the magical stuff folded up on the table.

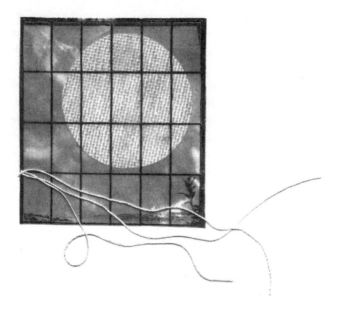

In the morning he brought it to the queen, who marvelled at the repair to her wondrous material. 'How did this happen? What did you do?'

'Not I, your majesty, but the moon herself. Your cloth is made of moonlight.'

The queen was amazed. 'Now my daughter can get married! Prepare for a wedding!' she called to her servants. They scurried to do her bidding.

'What can I give you in return for not only restoring our heir-loom, but revealing its secret?'

Yankel told the queen of his quest. 'If I could cut a small piece off the bottom of the material, that would be payment enough.'

The queen agreed and watched as Yankel cut off a tiny shimmering corner. She filled his pack with food and his pockets with silver and gold. He set off on his long journey home with the city ringing with bells, the princess was getting married.

Every night Yankel took the square of cloth out of his pocket and turned it in the moonlight. Every night the cloth grew larger and longer. It doubled, tripled, quadrupled in size. He folded it up and put it in his pocket.

His journey back was much easier because of the gold the queen had given him. Even so, the year was nearly up when he stepped into the tailors' union hall.

They had almost given up on him. Imagine their surprise when he walked in.

And then their astonishment that, of all people, Yankel had succeeded!

He handed them the material. The most successful tailors insisted that they be the ones trusted to cut the pattern. They pushed their favourites to help with the sewing. Everyone wanted to be the one chosen. Their voices grew louder and louder.

Until one old man waved them down.

'There is only one person who has the right to cut this cloth.'

'Yes!' they all shouted, thinking, hoping he meant them.

'Only one person who deserves to cut this cloth.'

'Yes!' This time fewer thought he meant them.

'Yankel!'

'Yes!' they all shouted. 'Yankel!'

Pleased and worried at the same time, Yankel protested but the tailors in the union hall were agreed. Under their supervision, Yankel cut the pattern and began the sewing. Everyone helped. Yankel was now a respected tailor.

As the year ended, the garment was ready. The tailors handed it to the designers. The designers handed it to the sun. The sun handed it to the moon, who put it on straightaway.

It fitted her perfectly.

And that is why, some nights when it is very cold, you can see a halo around the moon, her garment keeping her warm no matter what time of the month it is.

BRADFORD

Bradford Jewry came into its own in the 1880s. Many Jews owned the textile mills and helped make Bradford the wool capital of Britain.

Rudi Leavor came to Bradford with his parents and younger sister Winnie as a refugee from Nazi Germany in 1937 aged 11, having been raised in Berlin. He spent his career as a dentist, having a successful practice in Heckmondwike, near Batley. He was made President and Chairman of the Bradford Synagogue in 1975. He lives in Bradford with his wife Marianne. He put this memory up on the Bradford Jewish Community website.

RUDI'S CAKE

Rudi and his father visited Leeds, a larger town than Bradford about 15km away, to visit a dental depot not long after they arrived. Afterwards, as a special treat because money was very scarce in those days, they went to a café and ordered some coffee and cakes. The waitress brought a plate of small cakes that, she said, cost four pence. They each took a cake. Rudi ate his cake quickly and helped himself to another, which soon went the way of the first as it was so small. When that too was gone Rudi reached for another. His father had already looked at him in surprise when he took the second piece. But when Rudi took the third, he remonstrated with his son, 'What are you doing? I don't have so much money with us.'

Rudi reddened. 'But there are at least ten pieces on the plate and it only cost four pence a plate. Surely I could eat three pieces?'

'No, son, no,' said his father. 'Each piece of cake costs four pence. You have eaten eight pence worth already. Together with mine, that's a shilling before we add in the coffee.'

Rudi put the third piece back on the plate as quickly as he could.

COUNTING THE COST

In a kosher restaurant on the other side of Bradford a man was finishing his meal of main course, meat and potatoes, and pudding. He called for his bill. The main course was £7 and the pudding was £7. He gave the woman on the till £15. He was surprised to get £4 in change.

Being honest, he queried it with the cashier.

'But my main course was £7 and the sweet £7, that makes £14.'

'No, it makes £11,' the woman insisted. The man was now curious.

'How do you get that then?' he asked.

'Well, I have four children from my first husband. And my man has four children from his first marriage. We have three children from our marriage. So, both of us have seven children of our own. But in our house, there are only eleven children.' She was triumphant as she said, 'It's obvious! Seven and seven make eleven, not fourteen!'

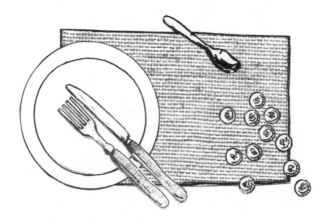

York

Clifford's Tower

It was the grandest procession yet. Richard I was on his way to be crowned at Westminster Abbey in September 1189. Crowds thronged the route. All his subjects wanted to take part, even his Jews. The Jews were under the direct rule of the king. As they had come into England with William the Conqueror, they owed no allegiance to any lord or feudal manor. They were the king's own and were taxed by him as such. Whenever he wanted money he turned to his Jews and levied a new tax on them. They had paid for a great deal of the festivities at Westminster and they wanted to see the king crowned.

Richard, however, decided that paying for it was one thing, seeing it was another. He forbade the Jews to attend the ceremony. He also forbade all women from coming to his investiture. Whilst the women turned away and didn't venture out, some of the richest Jews in the country arrived bringing presents on such a joyous occasion. This enraged the throng, already excited by the thought of the Crusade Richard was about to embark on, who stripped the Jews and beat them. One, Benedict of York, the richest Jew in England, died from his injuries.

Although Richard was understandably annoyed at the loss of his banker, it didn't stop the anti-Semitic riots that spread through the country. Up in York, they were mourning the loss of Benedict. On 16 March 1190 rioting had reached York.

Benedict's stone house on Spen Lane was attacked, its straw roof set ablaze. Most of the Jews lived and worked in Coney Street, Jubbergate and Pavement, the commercial centre of York. The rioters rampaged through those streets. Fearing the strength of the mob, the Jewish community took refuge in the royal keep, where Clifford's Tower now stands.

The local gentry, all of whom had borrowed money from the Jews of York, pondered how to turn this to their advantage. Richard Malebisse, William Percy, Marmeduke Darell and Philip de Fauconberg had borrowed against the expectation of royal appointments in the new king's entourage. Sadly for them and the Jews of York, these didn't materialise, so they were out of pocket. They encouraged the rioters, mainly their men, to burn the Jews' houses and kill any Jew they came across.

In the royal wooden keep, the 150 Jews didn't know whom to trust. They had heard of the violence done to Benedict's body in the sight of the king. They knew the men were from the local lords. So when the royal constable tried to get into the castle, they repulsed him and slammed the huge plank down, locking him out. He was incensed, who were they to deny him his rightful place?

He called for force to break into the castle. The knights arrived with their siege engines. Things were spiralling out of control. A fiery priest who wandered from parish to parish turned up, spouting inflammatory nonsense. Then a stone fell from the walls of the keep, killing the priest. There was no stopping the mob now.

Inside, the Jews gathered together. They could see no way of getting out of the keep safely.

'We could ask them to let the women and children go free,' said one.

'They'd never let them live, listen to them baying for our blood,' said another.

'Perhaps if we converted and became baptised Christians, they'd spare us,' cried a third.

'Didn't help Benedict, did it? He still died after his conversion.'

Josce, a wealthy member of the community, and Rabbi Yomtob, who had recently come from Joigny in France, conferred together.

'I admit this isn't what I thought I was coming to, when I accepted your offer to lecture in York.'

'I'm sorry. This wasn't what I had in mind either. Do you see a way out? I must say that forcible baptism doesn't consume me with hope.'

The two men spoke quietly, as the hall was filled with the whole of the York community, men, women and children. The women held on to their children, shushing them, cuddling them, weeping quietly. A lot of the men gathered together to pray.

Josce and Rabbi Yomtob agreed a plan. They called for silence.

'My friends, we have to have the courage of those at Masada and Gamla. They too faced death and defilement by the Romans or forcible conversion. We know from bitter experience that even if we do convert, they will never let us forget who we are and eventually they will kill us. We cannot kill them; we have no weapons. We cannot stop them. There is only one thing we can do. We can stop them defiling us.'

Josce stopped, his heart was beating fast. Who was he to ask this of others?

'Like those at Masada, we will kill ourselves before we are captured. Those last souls will set the place afire, so the mob cannot hurt our bodies, before they commit suicide themselves. We are martyrs for God.' Rabbi Yomtob spoke strongly. He could see no other way.

'Hold on, Rabbi, not all of us agree. I'm happy to take my chances with baptism.'

'Those of you who want to go down that road, please wait until we have finished before you open the door.' Josce was patient but clear.

The hall filled with murmurs as mothers begged forgiveness from their children. They helped each other to commit suicide. Soon the hall was silent. Josce and Rabbi Yomtob set fire to the hall before the few who wanted to convert opened the doors. Josce and Rabbi Yomtob took their own lives as the raging crowd roared in. Those who asked to convert were run down and trampled on. No one was left alive. The keep burned to the ground.

Richard Malebisse, William Percy, Marmeduke Darell and Philip de Fauconberg ran to York Minster. They removed the deeds and bonds deposited there for safekeeping by the Jews. To stop the king claiming the Jews' property and debts owed to them, they burned all the documents. Then they volunteered for the Crusade and left England. Richard was angry. Things had gone too far. He held a royal inquest, which fined the city of York, but he too was already on the Continent, heading for the Holy Land.

In 1990 English Heritage and the American Jewish Foundation planted the hill below Clifford's Tower with a special type of daffodil. These have six petals and bloom in mid-March, a yellow star of David, commemorating the massacre of York's Jewry.

There is a story that a *cherem*, a ban, was placed on York in memory of the massacre. No Jew would eat or stay overnight in York. Five years later the community was established again but by the expulsion in 1290 there were only six Jewish houses left. Not until 1939, when 118 refugees found safety in the city, were there so many Jews in York again.

NEWCASTLE

Newcastle Jews had lived on Silver Street, previously known as Jew Gate, until they were expelled in 1290. Modern Jewish Newcastle started in the early 1830s.

Professional people from the Continent arrived and soon built a synagogue. By the time the Jews from Eastern Europe arrived the community was well established. Eventually the more Hassidic moved across the Tyne to Gateshead, where they built *yeshivot* for boys and seminaries for girls to study the Torah. The two communities rub along, like *mechutn*, related by marriage. The Hassidim love *nigunim*, wordless songs in praise of God.

THE NIGUN

A wealthy merchant from Newcastle wanted a learned *yeshiva bocher* for a son-in-law. He chose from among many students in the Gateshead Yeshiva, Itzik the dreamer. As a test, he gave Itzik £50 to go to Sunderland and buy cloth.

Itzik set off with the money. Along the way he pondered the wonder of the universe created by HaShem, the cold North Sea, the wheeling seagulls, the heather on the moors and the green fields. He looked at the sheep in the field nearby with a smile. Then he heard the shepherd play a haunting tune on his flute.

'I must have that tune,' he said, and hopped over the drystone wall to get to the shepherd.

'Will you teach me that tune?'

'Nothing comes from nothing,' said the shepherd. 'Pay me and I will.'

'How much?'

The shepherd cast a knowledgeable eye over Itzik. He recognised the kind of dreamer he was and said, '£10.'

'Done.'

The shepherd taught Itzik the tune 'yam dai dai diddle diddle di di dai dai'.

Itzik went off happily humming the *nigun*. He thought how pleased his betrothed would be to sing this *nigun* on Shabbos when they were married. So busy was he, singing the tune, he didn't look where he was going and tripped over a stone in the road.

Oy! The tune went straight out of his head. No matter how he tried he couldn't get it back. What to do? What to do? There was only one thing to do … he went back to the shepherd and asked for the tune again.

The shepherd said, 'You bought the tune for one time only. I have to charge you for teaching you the tune again.'

Itzik didn't hesitate, 'I need the tune, I'll pay your price.'

'Fine,' said the shepherd, '£20.'

'Done.'

The shepherd taught Itzik the tune again, 'yam dai dai diddle diddle di di dai dai'. This time Itzik didn't leave until he was sure he had the *nigun* in his head.

Smiling, he continued on his way to Sunderland and his business. He still had £20. He was sure he could buy enough good cloth to make his prospective father-in-law happy.

Then, out of nowhere, came a plaintive melody. Itzik's heart lifted at the sound. Oh, this one complemented the tune he had already, he had to have it. He searched for the source and found a fiddler leaning against a tumbledown hut, playing 'chiri biri bom chiri biri bom chiri biri biri chiri biri chiri biri bom bom bim bom'.

'Will you sell me that tune?' asked Itzik.

The fiddler looked Itzik up and down. He saw at once what a dreamer he was.

'Yes, but it'll cost you.'

'I don't care,' answered Itzik. 'How much?'

'£20!'

'Done!'

This time Itzik didn't leave until the melody was locked into his head. Having spent all the money, he turned around and went home.

The merchant stared out of his window. He saw Itzik walking down the road. There were no parcels on his back or in his arms. He didn't trundle a barrow with the goods in. The merchant ran out of his house and stopped Itzik in the street.

'What are you doing back here so soon? Have you spent the money? Did you buy cloth? What have you spent the money on you no-goodnik?'

Itzik looked at his future father-in-law calmly. He nodded his head. 'Yes, yes, I spent the money. You'll be so pleased when you know what I have bought.'

The merchant was taken aback. 'I'll be pleased? So, tell me, *khokhom*, what I'll be pleased with?'

'First,' said Itzik, 'I bought this tune.' He opened his mouth and sang, 'Yam dai dai diddle diddle di di dai dai. Isn't it lovely? Yam dai dai diddle diddle di di dai dai.'

'And how much did this wonder cost you?' asked the merchant in a dangerous tone, but Itzik was oblivious.

'A snip at £30!'

'£30!' The merchant struggled to keep himself from shouting at the hapless fellow. 'And what, may I ask, did you spend the other £20 on? Something equally fabulous?'

'Why, yes,' smiled Itzik and proceeded to sing the other tune. 'Chiri biri bom chiri biri bom chiri biri biri chiri biri chiri biri bom bom bim bom. I think it's worth every penny.' He then sang the first tune again, followed by the second and again with the first.

The merchant went back into his house and slammed the door. He forbade his daughter to even think of a *yeshiva bocher* as a husband. She would have an accountant and like it.

The Yeshiva found a match for Itzik and every Friday night after the Shabbos candles were lit and he and his wife had eaten they sang his *nigun*, happy in their wonder of the glory of HaShem's creation.

Yam dai dai diddle diddle di di dai dai.
Yam dai dai diddle diddle di di dai dai.
Chiri biri bom chiri biri bom
chiri biri biri chiri biri chiri biri bom bom bim bom.
Yam dai dai diddle diddle di di dai dai.
Yam dai dai diddle diddle di di dai dai.

☙❧

Bohemian Jewish merchants first arrived in Sunderland around 1750. A hundred years later when the North East exported coal to the eastern Baltic, Polish Jews paid for passage to Sunderland to fill the empty vessels coming back.

A man was on the Friday train from Newcastle to Sunderland. A young *yeshiva bocher* came and sat next to him. The young man asked him what the time was. The older man ignored him. After waiting a while, the young man asked again. The older man still ignored him. The young man asked a third time. Sighing, the older man told him the time.

'Why didn't you tell me the first time?'

'Well, when we get to Sunderland, it's late and close to Shabbos. You won't know anyone, so I'll take you home. You'll meet my family. You'll meet my daughter who is *keynahora*, beautiful. You'll fall in love and want to marry her. Do I want a son-in-law who can't afford a watch?'

EDINBURGH

Edinburgh University had for some time in the 1600s several professors of Hebrew who were converted Jews. However, the first professing Jew known to have lived and worked in Edinburgh was David Brown. He had applied for permission from the city burgesses so he could continue to trade. Licence was granted in 1691 for him to reside and trade in Edinburgh but not as a burgess. But the precedent had been set: strangers of birth and religion were welcome in Edinburgh and indeed in Scotland. So much so that it was only a few years later in 1698 that a Jew, Moses Mosias, was admitted to the register of burgesses of Edinburgh. It was noted dryly that if Mosias would convert he could enter the rolls, gratis.

From then on, the Jewish population of Edinburgh slowly grew. The first Jewish doctor to graduate from the university was Dr Joseph Hart Myers in 1779. He was born in America but brought up in Scotland. He went on to have a glittering career both professionally and within his religion. Other professions were chiropodists like Heyman or Herman Lion, who bought the first plot in the city for Jewish burial in 1795, dentists, merchants and traders. There was a small group of waterproofers as well as embroiderers, tailors, pressers and cutters. Synagogues were founded and closed.

One of Shimon bar Yochai's sayings was: There are three crowns – the crown of the Law, the crown of the priesthood, and the crown of kingship; but the crown of a good name excels them all. [Seder Nezīqīn (Pirķe Avot 4:13)]

This is true of Rabbi Dr Salis Daiches, the Rabbi of Edinburgh in 1919–45. His interest in Hume and Scotland was lifelong, as was his meld of traditional Judaism and secular study. There is a street in Edinburgh named Daiches Braes after him; it was one of the first streets in Britain named for a Rabbi. Rabbi Daiches loved the Highlands and walking among the banks and braes. He once told of coming across a Jewish tailor in Wester Ross who only spoke Gaelic and Yiddish. A lot of Rabbi Daiches' congregants spoke Scots–Yiddish, impenetrable to many, whereas Rabbi Daiches' English was impeccable. According to his son, he spoke the accentless English of the eighteenth century. He spoke French with a German accent and German; only speaking Yiddish, his *mama-loshen* (mother tongue), when he had to. He brought together the disparate Jewish communities of Edinburgh under one roof and the eventual building in Salisbury Road.

Here is another well-known story, from Palestine, set this time in the Highlands of Scotland where Rabbi Daiches loved to roam.

THE CORPSE BRIDE

Once, three young men were 'strolling' in the Highlands. Their hearts were full as one of them, Reuben, was getting married the next day. They had taken a little more of the local *uisge* (whisky) than usual so were rather merry. They tripped and stumbled their way along the bank of a stream, laughing and joking. Reuben, in the midst of a giggle, tumbled over tree roots exposed above the ground.

'Look,' he snickered, 'this root looks like a finger, doesn't it, guys?'

'Well, why don't you try the ring on it?' suggested his friend, Sam. 'I have it with me. I didn't want to lose it.' He took the box out of his pocket and offered it to Reuben.

Reuben took the ring out of the box and held it over the woody digit. The gold ring sent a surge of power into the ground and something awoke. As Reuben slipped the ring over the finger he collapsed in laughter. His friends laughed with him. None of them noticed the shiver that travelled up the finger.

'Good chance to practise your words, Reuben. Get your teeth in order,' said Barney, 'so you don't make a fool of yourself, stumbling

on the Hebrew tomorrow.' The three of them hooted and rolled on the bank. Barney took out his flask and the three of them had another swig each.

'Okay,' said Reuben, wiping his mouth, 'here goes. *Harei at m'kudeshet li b'taba'at zo k'dat Mosheh v'Yisrael .*'*

'Oh brilliant, not a mistake. You'll knock it out of the park tomorrow,' said Sam.

---

* 'Behold you [fem.] are consecrated unto me, with this ring, according to the Law of Moses and Israel.'

'Yeah, well done, mate,' said Barney, 'you won't need the rabbi's help.'

Reuben smiled a rather gassy smile. Then his eyes grew larger. He scrambled back, desperate to get away. The ground shook. The force was so strong that the tree creaked as it fell to the side. A gaping hole opened up and from it shot a figure into the sky.

It swooped around until it saw the three lads, gobsmacked, on the ground. The figure arrowed down to them. As it came closer, the lads saw the figure was a woman, a half-decomposed woman. They screamed. Reuben fainted.

The woman landed and hobbled towards them. 'Which one of you is my husband? Who put the ring on my finger? Who said the words?' She swivelled her head to look at them.

The boys gagged. One of her eyes was hanging by a thread on her cheek. Green and white maggots danced across her skin. Her dress was in rags, covering what little flesh she had left.

Barney and Sam pointed to Reuben, lying on the ground, then did what best friends do: they legged it back to the village as fast as possible. Reuben opened his eyes and gazed in horror at the creature in front of him.

'You said the blessing, making me yours in the sight of two witnesses. We are married! How I've longed for this moment. I will never let you go.' She moved towards him; arms outstretched.

'Wait for me, lads!' Reuben shouted as he ran after them.

Bleary eyed, Sam and Barney knocked on Reuben's door late the next morning. Reuben opened the door, shushing them. His head was banging. The boys got him ready for his wedding and walked him down to the village square in the afternoon, where the wedding canopy had been set up. The whole village had turned up to see a Jewish wedding in a Scottish village. So unusual, so exotic. A lone piper played klezmer melodies.

The rabbi was standing under the canopy, waiting. Reuben and his friends walked carefully down to the canopy. Becky, veiled, walked down to the canopy escorted by her parents holding candles. She began her seven circles of Reuben to bind him to her. She didn't get far.

A screech seared the sky. Everyone looked at the piper, who shook his head. Then they noticed something hurtling towards the canopy and the figures standing there.

'He is my husband. He is not free to marry. We are wed.' The corpse bride held up her bony finger where the gold ring glinted. She smiled out of the side of her mouth still fleshed. Reuben realised he hadn't had a nightmare and promptly fainted. Becky, made of sterner stuff, walked to a chair and sat down. Her parents sat beside her. The villagers were rapt. This was better than the visiting theatre groups.

The rabbi took a moment. The corpse bride paced up and down until Reuben was brought round.

'He put a ring on my finger. He said the vow in front of witnesses. We are married.' The corpse bride was triumphant. 'I can have my pleasure at last.'

The rabbi questioned Sam and Barney. They agreed and Reuben looked sickly.

'You are indeed married,' said the rabbi. 'You will have to get a *get* (a divorce) before you can marry Becky now.'

The audience gasped.

'Hold on a minute,' said Becky's father. 'We had an agreement, a contract. Reuben's father and I signed the agreement when the two were babies.'

'Ah,' said the rabbi, 'that changes things. The agreement was first, so the ring and the vow become null and void.'

A huge sigh sounded from the bagpipe. The piper turned red.

The corpse bride was having none of it. 'If he is not married to me and I have the pleasure of knowing the marriage bed then I will be in the bed every night. Between him and his wife. Every night.'

A gasp from the audience came again. Who knew that attending a Jewish wedding would be such high drama?

The rabbi thought and then he pulled Reuben aside. They had a low-voiced, intense conversation. Reuben turned white and fainted.

Not long afterwards Becky insisted that Reuben undergo a thorough decontamination cleansing, which he was happy to do. He'd found a few green maggots tangled in his beard and a long fingernail in one of his side curls. When he went to the *mikveh* on the eve of their reconvened wedding, he scrubbed himself raw before entering the water. The rabbi intoned a special blessing for services beyond.

The rabbi buried the corpse bride in a quiet corner of the Jewish part of Edinburgh's Piershill Cemetery. The bride was buried with a smile on her lopsided face. The piper played a highland lament for her followed by a *vigdis*, a Yiddish lullaby.

DUNDEE

Wealthy Jewish textile merchants from Germany came to Dundee in the mid-1800s to establish trade with the jute producers and took up residence. Dundee was booming. Not long after, Polish and Russian Jews arrived, fleeing the pogroms and settled near the Irish immigrants, fleeing the potato famine. A synagogue was built in Murrygate Street in 1874 and another one in Ward Road in the late 1870s. The two congregations remained separate until 1885, when they merged. No one knows, now, why they did so. Perhaps this story from Poland may give us a clue. There is a belief that babies have the knowledge of their souls' past lives while in the womb, but just before birth the angels place a finger under the baby's nose on their top lip and remove it.

THE ANGELS' STORYTELLER

Once there was a rabbi and his wife who were childless. They longed for a child of their own and prayed long and hard. The rabbi consoled his wife with the story of Sarah, Abraham's wife, who was 90 when she conceived their son, Isaac. The rabbi's wife hoped she would not have to wait until she was 90. She prayed even harder, taking the story of Hannah who prayed for a son at Shilo as her guide. She stood and prayed silently, swaying on her feet for hours at a time.

One night the rabbi's wife dreamed she was visited by the angel Lailah, who promised her a child within the coming year. It was a special child they were to name Samuel. The rabbi's wife woke

with hope in her heart and told her husband. The pair of them
were overjoyed.

'You see, I'm like Hannah, who had a son called Samuel, not
Sarah,' the rabbi's wife said.

'Yes, yes, you were right. I, thank God, was wrong. How wonderful! The world is richer already,' said the rabbi.

The child was born in due time. A boy! The parents *kvelled*,
such a miracle! And the boy … his face was glowing.
At his *bris*, he was named Samuel. The wine touched his lips and
he opened his mouth and began to talk. In whole sentences! The
rabbi, his wife and guests were astonished.

Samuel told his parents to gather the congregation together.
Not only from his *shul*, but also from the other *shul*, the one they
didn't go to.

The whole Jewish community, as small as it was, managed to
squeeze into the rabbi's *shul*. The rabbi and his wife sat on chairs
on the *bimah*, Samuel held securely in his mother's arms. Everyone
waited, wanting to hear the wonder child. When all was quiet
Samuel spoke.

He told the assembled congregants that in the last world he had
been a storyteller. Unfortunately, he had died before he could finish
his last story. The angels, who had been listening in, wanted to know
the end of the story. They had petitioned God for Samuel to return
and finish the story for them. God had listened to them and had
listened to the prayers and entreaties of the rabbi's wife. He decided
to grant both sets of prayers. Three hundred years after the story had
begun, it was time for the ending to be heard on earth.

The people cried out. Not just the ending! They needed to hear the
whole story the angels found so fascinating. The rabbi and his wife
looked at each other and smiled. This child of theirs was amazing.

As the sun went down, the congregants listened. The moon came
up and the congregants listened. Samuel told the story through
the night. Angels perched in the rafters of the *shul*, hanging on
every word.

When Samuel brought the story to its conclusion, a sigh of pleasure dropped down from the top to the bottom of the building. The people sat back on the hard benches, in sheer delight. The angels wafted their wings, creating a breeze filled with the scent of Gan Eden.

Lailah flew down to the *bimah* where the rabbi and his wife sat, their faces glowing with pride in their son. She smiled at the baby boy and touched him on his upper lip under his nose.

Samuel opened his eyes wide as she did so. He opened his mouth to speak and … gurgled.

From then on Samuel grew as a normal human baby. He learned to speak as a normal human child. But the rabbi and his wife never forgot the miracle of his birth. Or his storytelling.

The congregants from the two shuls never forgot the story either. They had shared something during that night that they didn't want to relinquish. They held a meeting and decided to stay together. The *shul* they made their collective home was … Samuel's father's. And they never regretted it.

GLASGOW

From the 1860s to the 1940s, the Gorbals of Glasgow heard more Yiddish than English. Hoardings and shop signs were in Yiddish, the butchers, bakers and grocers were Jewish. Even the fish was Yiddish, herring in brine, herring in barrels, herring! Far from Latvia, Lithuania and Poland and other parts of the Russian Empire, the Jews of Scotland discovered a fish that would take the brine and the smoking cure so familiar to them, the king of fish, the salmon. Luckily for them, salmon is kosher with fins and scales, unlike the Russian sturgeon from whom caviar was collected. The word for salmon in Yiddish is *lachs*. Here's a tongue-twister for you: So many *lachs* in the lochs in Scotland once smoked become *lox*.

Soon smoked salmon was on the menu and sent down to London. They called it the London cure but we know different, don't we? Some of the Jews travelled on to New York, taking with them their fish. Not herring, but ... *lox*! A bagel with a *schmear* of cream cheese and *lox*, so tasty.

Glasgow grew. Its diverse Jewish community of furriers, tailors, furniture makers, jewellers, textile merchants, optical and mathematical instrument makers, among others, built several synagogues with Garnethill being the first purpose-built and most enduring, now Grade I listed. The Giffnock and Newlands *shul* houses the twenty-two beautiful stained-glass windows from the defunct Queens Park *shul*. Jews were initially buried in the Glasgow necropolis, behind the gate inscribed with the words from Byron's Hebrew melody, 'Oh! weep for those that wept by Babel's stream.'

This story is based on Rabbi Juspa's in the seventeenth century.

Change the Place, Change the Luck

The families in the Gorbals were so poor that they had nowhere else to go but up.

Many saw their parents struggle to provide for the family and were determined not to be in want ever again.

Others saw Glasgow as a stepping stone on their journey to the *goldene medina* of America. They were desperate to leave Europe and all their tribulations behind them. They would have a new life in America. Things would be different.

Once there was a Jew called Berl, who suffered from bad luck. Nothing he did succeeded. Nothing he turned his hand to made a living. He despaired. He was the epitome of the Yiddish saying *mit der puter arop* (with the buttered side down). What was he to do?

It was the time when many Jews were migrating from Lithuania to America. Berl decided to leave his *shtetl* and try his luck in a new country. He walked and walked. No one would give him a lift and he was saving his money for his boat tickets. It was a long way to travel: Lithuania to Poland, Poland to Scotland, Scotland to New York.

After a long, hard journey, Berl arrived in Glasgow. He was surprised he had got this far without losing any limbs, the troubles he'd had. Knowing he would have to wait for some time for an entry visa, he looked for a room in a boarding house in the Gorbals.

Door after door shut in his face, the places were filled. There was no room.

Eventually, Berl knocked on a door in a tenement and was asked inside. As he climbed the worn stairs to the room he would be sharing, his heart filled with happiness that at long last something was going right.

His landlady knocked on the door of the room. It was opened immediately. A man stood there, his face beaming with joy.

'*Shalom aleichem*, come in, come in,' said the man. He shook Berl's hand with enthusiasm.

'I'm sorry,' said Berl, 'do I know you?'

'You mean you don't recognise me? I've been your companion for your whole life!'

'But who are you?'

'I'm your bad luck. You didn't think you could go to America and not take me with you, did you? I found this room here in Glasgow earlier today so we could travel on together, like always.'

Belfast

The earliest reference to the Jews in Ireland was in the year 1079. The Annals of Inisfallen record 'Five Jews came from over sea with gifts to Tairdelbach (king of Munster), and they were sent back again over sea.' They were probably merchants from Normandy where there was a secure Jewish community. Although there is a record of a Jewish tailor in Belfast in 1652, a Manuel Lightfoot, the Belfast community wasn't established properly until the 1850s.

In 1845 Daniel Jaffe, a linen merchant from Hamburg, landed in Belfast to establish business contacts. Within a decade he had his businesses up and running there. He'd moved his large family from Germany to Belfast and founded the first synagogue in Great Victoria Street. More Jewish families from Germany joined him. Due to the blockade of American ports during that country's Civil War, Belfast became the centre of international trade in linen and Daniel Jaffe was at the heart of the town's growth. After he died a fountain was erected in the centre of Belfast in his memory. His son, Otto, became the first Jewish Lord Mayor of Belfast.

This version of a story, found in the Mishnah, is from Germany.

Star Girl

Two angels were arguing in front of the throne of the Source. What was the subject of these angels' argument? Why man, of course.

Azazel said no son of Adam could be trusted to keep faith with God. Shemhazai disagreed. 'They are faithful, unlike some angels I can name.' He gave Azazel a dirty look.

Azazel puffed out his wings in anger. He brushed against the throne and the decorations around it shuddered. Shemhazai puffed out his wings in response, knocking the throne the other way.

One of the jewels came loose and rolled onto the floor.

Both angels lunged to catch it but it slipped out of their grasp and fell through the heavens.

Azazel and Shemhazai looked at each other. They knew they were for it.

Far below on earth, Istahar stared up at the night sky. She loved the stars that twinkled in the velvety black. How she longed to be up there with them, sparkling in the night. Suddenly she saw a flash across the sky. It was a falling star. Usually she closed her eyes as soon as she saw one and wished. Somehow, she knew not to close her eyes this time. She watched the star come closer and closer. It was falling into the orchard below the field she was in.

Istahar ran across the wet grass until she came to the apple trees. She searched for the glow of the star among the tangled branches. There! She saw it. Quickly she grabbed hold of the gnarled trunk and hoisted herself up. She stretched and managed to reach the star with her fingertips.

Back on the ground, she wiped the star clean of debris. Now she could see it was faceted like a jewel ... she'd expected points. As she turned it over a ball of light appeared in front of her. A mellifluous voice spoke from its depths.

'Be careful, child. What you hold is precious. Many will want to take it from you. Do not be deceived. Guard it well and your deepest desire will be granted.'

Istahar realised the ball of light was a manifestation of the *Shekhinah*, God's presence. She bowed and as she did so the light disappeared.

She left the orchard with the star jewel hidden in her pocket.

Azazel and Shemhazai descended to earth. They folded their wings so they were flat across their backs. They looked around with pleasure. The scenery was green, the girls were pretty, the water looked inviting. This was going to be easy. The rule not to get involved ... well ...

'All we have to do is get the jewel and take it back up to the Source.'

'Yes, I know, you don't have to keep on.'

'I'm going to bring it back.'

'No, I am.'

They continued to quarrel until they reached Istahar's house. The pull of the jewel was strong. 'Let's toss to see who tries to get it first,' said Shemhazai and was downcast when Azazel won.

Azazel, who had spent the morning with the pretty girls, was not at the top of his game when he approached Istahar.

He told her how important it was to return the jewel to the throne of the Creator. He told her how dangerous it was for her to keep it. He told her that it would be best for everyone if she gave it to him. He would look after it for her.

Istahar looked at Azazel. He was the epitome of cool with his dark good looks. He stood in the sunshine and smiled the smile that had all the pretty girls swooning. Istahar was made of sterner stuff. She remembered what the *Shekhinah* had said and looked closer. Azazel had no shadow! She didn't trust anyone who had no shadow, even if they were an angel. She only had his word for that.

She turned from him and walked away. Azazel ground his teeth. Shemhazai smiled as he stepped forward to take his turn.

Shemhazai talked to Istahar about being an angel. He opened his wings for her. He sang songs the angels sang only for the Source.

'Let me try your wings on and I'll give you the star jewel,' said Istahar. Shemhazai looked shocked.

'I've shared with you more than I should have, I can't do that,' he replied.

Istahar allowed Shemhazai a peek at the jewel. Shemhazai gulped.

'I've never done this before,' he said as he removed his wings from his back and fitted them to Istahar. Her face glowed as she opened the wings.

She thrust up and flew straight to God. She handed the jewel over. God granted her deepest wish and turned her into a star, where she is now, twinkling down on you and me.

As for Shemhazai and Azazel, what happened to them is another story.

Many inhabitants of the Jewish community in Belfast remembered with fondness the superstitions that abounded in the countries of their birth. Here, in the country that had taken them in as refugees, or economic migrants, or even plain business developers, those stories and attitudes were looked on with a quizzical eye. Who would believe that marrying the most unfortunate of people in a cemetery would reverse the encroachments of plague? Here in Belfast, where public health had come under the remit of the council determined to eradicate the causes of cholera and typhus after the epidemic of 1848, whitewashing houses and paving streets in the crowded city centre doing much to alleviate the problem, surely all that superstition was a thing of the past?

The Wedding in the Cemetery

The Jews of Cracow were suffering the effects of the plague. Many had died. Hope was lost. There was only one thing left to do. They organised the wedding of the poorest man in the community. He was a hunchback who would in normal circumstances not even have a chance of marriage, but because of the plague had been thrust into the position of *chosan*. The bride was decked out by the women. She was the daughter of an elderly couple who had protected her from marriage. Why would anyone marry her? With her eyes looking two ways at once, her mouth lopsided, she was enough to give anyone the runs. So here she was on the wrong side of 40, eking out a living by cleaning. The community gathered enough utensils to set the 'young' couple up in a small hut on the outskirts of town. And then they held the wedding in the cemetery, which was unusually by the synagogue. It was Friday afternoon and the whole congregation celebrated, hoping the end of the plague would come. They celebrated so hard they forgot that Shabbos started at sundown. Suddenly there was a loud crack and the cemetery split down the centre. The revellers were swallowed up like Korach* and his followers. You can still see the crack down the centre of the cemetery of the old synagogue in Cracow.

Aaron Shrage, a resident of the city, wrote in the *Belfast Jewish Record* in 1958 about his family town of Zborov, Galicia. He related how the small town had been subjected to the plague and nothing seemed to stem the numbers of deaths. Here is his story.

MOISHE THE WATER CARRIER

Moishe would wade into the river and fill his two wooden tubs, which he carried on a wooden yoke across his shoulders. From dawn to dusk, Moishe would ply his trade walking with full tubs into town and to the houses, then back again with empty ones to the river. Fridays he would work twice as hard to give the houses enough water to last them over Shabbos. In 1895 a cholera epidemic swept through the Ukraine and Eastern Galicia, including Aaron's town of Zborov.

---

* Korach had led a revolt against Moses and the ground opened up and swallowed them. Numbers 16:1–18:32

The houses were sealed off and no one was allowed in or out. Many died during the first week of the epidemic. Prayers were said in *shul*. Then when that didn't work, they went to the cemetery to pray at the graves of the *tsaddikim* (saints), asking them to intercede with the Almighty. And still the plague raged. So they measured the length of the cemetery with lengths of cotton, which they then made into candles and gave to the *shul* to burn. To no avail. There was one last hope, a wedding in the cemetery.

Who to marry? It had to be the poorest of the community, for the cost was borne by the community. One name came to mind immediately, Moishe the water carrier! But who would be the *kale* (the bride)? They cast around and latched on to Bayle, the deaf daughter of Lemel, another water carrier. Everyone contributed to setting up the happy couple.

The klezmer band played and led the procession to the cemetery, singing '*Malakh Hamoves*, Angel of Death, we're not frightened of you, we'll beat you yet', where the wedding canopy was set up between the graves.

But when did the epidemic cease? At the end of November, when there was a heavy snowfall that cleared the air and killed all the germs.

An influx of Jews from Eastern Europe running from the pogroms arrived in Belfast from the 1880s onwards. These Jews had no money, unlike the German Jews forty years earlier. These Jews moved into small terraced houses on the Lower Antrim Road just to the north of the city centre. They were more orthodox than the German Jews. They didn't like the way the services were run at the Great Victoria Street Synagogue. They didn't like each other. They didn't flavour their gefilte fish the same way; the Poles added sugar, the Litvaks salt. How could they come together in such a divided city as Belfast?

A man was stopped at a control point. He was asked his religion. 'I'm Jewish,' the man replied. 'Ah, but are you a Protestant Jew or a Catholic Jew?'

During the Troubles, the new synagogue further down the Antrim Road was a place where both sides could come and talk to each other and negotiate.

Millisle Farm, just outside Belfast, was bought by the Jewish community so teenage refugees from Nazi-occupied Germany and Austria could learn how to farm. The Kindertransport children arrived there after the Blitz on Belfast in 1941, a place of refuge for the German, Austrian and Czech Jewish children who came without their parents. The farm was run on kibbutz lines with everyone mucking in. The children were told stories on Shabbat when they all got together. How to raise a smile on the face of a child who had lost everything?

The tales of the people of Chelm, the village of fools, might have helped.

THE CAT AND THE BUTTER

A Chelmnik and his wife lived on a farm. His wife had spent all morning churning butter and had proudly set the butter on the table. She had gone out to fetch her husband to see the butter and returned to find the cat slinking out of the door. The pair stared at the table.

The butter had gone! There was one suspect. The Chelmnik caught the cat and brought it back. After some discussion, the wife thought she had churned a pound of butter.

Her man weighed the cat. It weighed a pound. 'Well, that's the butter,' he said, 'but where's the cat?'

DUBLIN

There had been isolated Jews in Ireland through the ages from 1039, including Joseph the Doctor in 1171 and mention of Jews around Dublin in 'Calendar of Documents Relating to Ireland' in 1286. A small Sephardi community had settled around 1500 but had dissolved through assimilation.

Sephardim had a long history in Ireland. William Annyas was the first Jewish mayor in Ireland, in Youghal, Cork, in 1555. And just in case that was a mistake, Francis Annyas was elected mayor in Youghal in 1569, 1576 and 1581. Both men, Sephardi Jews, lived in County Cork with their families and no others.

When the Jews were allowed to resettle in the 1660s the Sephardim returned to Dublin, with the first synagogue in Marlborough Street in the yard of the glass works.

By 1738 a cemetery had been acquired in Drumcondra. Financial aid was sought from their Ashkenazi brethren in England to maintain it but help came instead from Bevis Marks Sephardi Synagogue in London, where the deeds to the cemetery are still to be found.

The Sephardim were used to crossing delicate borders. They had moved between Andalusia and Castile as well as Spain and Portugal. Here is one of the Sephardi trickster tales about crossing borders that echoes down five hundred years to an island with its own border in the twentieth century.

MICK AND HIS DONKEYS

Mick walked his train of donkeys to the checkpost. Every month he arrived from Belfast with his donkeys laden with goods to be traded in the south. Every month the border guard meticulously searched every inch of baggage. Mick picked his teeth with a sliver of wood as the border guard unpacked the goods and checked them off against the bill of lading. The border guard sorrowfully watched Mick pack them all back up and load them on the donkeys to continue on his way to Dublin and beyond. He grimaced as Mick would turn and give a little wave goodbye.

This went on for years. Scarcely a month went by without Mick turning up with his donkey train loaded with legitimate goods. The guard had resigned himself never to find the smuggled goods he knew in his bones that Mick was moving across the border. But he continued to go through the farce, month on month.

One day the border guard spoke to Mick as he began to walk his newly loaded donkeys over the border.

'Tell me, Mick, it's my last day. I know you've been smuggling something all these years. Please, as it's my last day, please tell me how you've been doing it.'

Mick laughed as he continued across the border. He turned around from the other side.

'I've been smuggling donkeys!'

The majority of Jews who came to Dublin in the 1880s were Ashkenazi, fleeing the pogroms and the expulsion from the Pale of Settlement.

The Jews who settled in Lower Clanbrassil Street on the south side of the River Liffey were mainly those from Lithuania and lived in the same style they had before, in cramped houses with simple shops in the front rooms of their houses. They were poor and illiterate, but hardworking with a great sense of community. This area of Portobello was known as Little Jerusalem because of the many Jews who settled around Hibernian Building and surrounding streets; perhaps one of the reasons that James Joyce placed Leopold Bloom in Clanbrassil Street.

This story is originally from Eastern Europe.

THE MIRACLE OF HANUKAH

The houses of Lower Clanbrassil Street were full of large families, six or more children, with parents who worked hard but gained little. They had to scrape together every penny to put food on the table. So it was not surprising when the festival of Hanukah came around that there was nothing to spare for a *menorah* and thoughts of Hanukah *gelt* were far away.

The children in one house had heard of the metal *menorah* left behind in the rush to get out of the way of the boots and beatings coming for their parents. How they had to pack in a hurry. They knew there was no money to spare, especially since their father was away on the road, selling. But they had been to *cheder* in the Heytesbury Street *shteibl* and had been stirred by the story of the Maccabees who had rid the Temple in Jerusalem of idols, lighting the *menorah* with oil that lasted for eight days instead of one, rededicating the Temple to God.

'You should light the *menorah* in the window of your house,' they'd been told by their enthusiastic young teacher. 'Every family should do it, for each of the eight nights, to remind us of the miracle.'

What could they use to make a *menorah* though? The children, all seven of them, searched the house for stubs of candles.

'Do we have to let the candles burn right down?' asked one of the youngest.

'Yes,' said the oldest. 'Each night there must be new candles to light or it won't be like the Maccabees.'

The children wondered if that meant they would get a miracle too and cut the stubs into enough tiny candles to last the eight days of the festival.

Mother called them to get the potatoes out of the sack in the back yard. She wanted to make potato *kugel* for the holiday. She knew her much-used oil wasn't enough to fry *latkes* (potato pancakes) for the week even though they were traditional. A *kugel*, eked out with a handful of flour, an onion and an egg, would go much further.

The children scrabbled in the bottom of the sack, finding four small green and black potatoes withering at the bottom. Their mother shook her head at the waste. She couldn't feed her children on them. She sighed. She would buy a new small sack of potatoes with her last pennies. She would do without the onion. The children wouldn't miss what they hadn't had.

'Can we use them to put our candles in?' asked the children, holding out the small offerings. With a yes, they set to and cut each potato in half. Then the eldest cored a small hole in the centre of each half. Soon eight potato candle holders were ready.

'But where is the *shammas*?' asked the youngest. 'We need a *shammas* to light the others. Our teacher said so.'

The children looked for another potato too small for peeling. The oldest held the ankles of the youngest as she delved head first into the sack. Her tiny fingers found a small nub of a tuber in the corner trapped among the weave. She came out triumphant, holding it aloft as if it were the cruse of oil found by the boy among the ruins of the Temple.

The oldest pursed his lips. He would have to be very careful in coring the hole for the candle in this potato. One slip and the whole thing would disintegrate. All the children clapped when he was done. He felt very proud.

They begged a small narrow tin tray off their mother and arranged the potato shells in a row with the *shammas* just squeezing in in front. They set it in the window of their house, ready for Hanukah.

The first night came and the children stood at the window watching as their father lit the tiny *shammas*. He held it up and sang the blessings before lighting the first candle. As the whole family watched the tiny candles burn to nothing, they sang the traditional hymn, *Ma'oz Tzur* (Rock of Ages), which told of the story of Hanukah to same melody it had been sung to for hundreds of years.

Every night the candles were lit, the song sung while the candles burned down and the *kugel* eaten.

By the fifth night the mother was at her wits end. Her flour was nearly finished. Her husband had left to sell again, leaving her with two coppers to last the week. As she grated the potato for the *kugel* she wished it was bigger. She had been making the *kugel*

smaller and smaller as the week went on. She had borrowed this egg from a neighbour, promising to replace it, who knew when. Her neighbour had smiled and handed over the egg without a murmur. That's how it was in Clanbrassil Street.

The family gathered round the potato shell *menorah* to light the candles. The oldest did the honours in place of his father. The children's face shone in the window lit by six candles as they sang.

Suddenly there was a knock on the door. An old man stood there.

'I saw the light from your *menorah*. I'm a stranger in Dublin and I was looking for a friendly *heimishe* place. Your *menorah* drew me, it was the most beautiful in the whole street. I need a place to stay the night. I can pay.' He held out three copper coins.

The mother thanked God for the miracle and asked the old man in. She quickly divided the *kugel* up into nine portions. Of course, they were not equal. The old man got the most and the children got the rest according to their age. The mother saved the tiny burnt corner crust for herself. She was used to doing without.

While the old man entertained the children with stories of Hanukah in the past and far away from Ireland, she made up a bed for him. He smiled and laughed with the children, his cheeks rosy with joy as they told him how they had made the *menorah* that had caught his attention.

In the morning, he was gone. A silver coin was left on the table. She could replace her neighbour's egg and buy an onion … no two, she thought and still have some over! She was so happy.

She went to the flour bin. It was brimming. The sack of potatoes seemed to be fuller than before. The mother put her hand into the sack and found a small bag. She pulled it out. A label was tied around its neck. In Yiddish it said, *Hanukah gelt* for the children. Inside were seven copper coins. One for each child.

The last three nights of Hanukah were filled with joy as the children watched the candles burn in their potato *menorah*. The mother was sure their visitor had been Elijah the Prophet, but she didn't tell the children as she gave them potato and onion *kugel* each night.

Dublin's Jewish community grew and prospered. The parents might have been illiterate but the next generation made education their way out of poverty. The families moved out of Little Jerusalem into the more prestigious area of Terenure and surrounds, and finally various synagogues merged to form the Dublin Hebrew congregation.

The first Chief Rabbi of Ireland (1921–36) was Rabbi Dr Yitzhak haLevi Herzog, whose son, Chaim, was born in Belfast and brought up in Dublin. Chaim went on to become the sixth President of Israel, while his father was the first Ashkenazi Chief Rabbi of Israel, having been the Chief Rabbi of the British Mandate in Palestine. Chaim Herzog retained close links with Ireland, presenting a sculpture in honour of the fifth president of Ireland, Cearbhall O Dalaigh, which is in Sneem Sculture Park, Co. Kerry.

This story is from Poland, where Rabbi Dr Herzog was born.

THE GILGUL

A *gilgul* is … what do you think? A trapped spirit? A demon? A lost soul? Listen to this story and see if you can decide.

Once there was a carpenter who needed to choose his next tree to be cut down. He was running out of seasoned timber and he knew he had to leave the tree at least a year after cutting.

It was a fine day when he and his daughter walked in the forest looking at the various trees that grew there. Between them they marked several possible trees. The carpenter cut down one while his daughter collected twigs, bundling them up for firewood. They went home tired but satisfied.

A week or so later his daughter started acting strangely. She had always been a happy girl but now she showed such a face to everyone. If she glowered at them, they thought themselves lucky! She refused to do her chores around the house and threw things at her brothers. She snarled and spat. In short, she made everyone's life a misery.

Her worried parents didn't know what to do. It got even worse when one day a man's voice came out of the girl's mouth.

'Take me to a rabbi,' the voice demanded. Not once, not twice. 'I am a *gilgul*. I need to see a rabbi!'

Well, the carpenter and his wife lived a long way from the nearest rabbi. Besides, it would be expensive to travel all that way. The carpenter decided to pretend to be the rabbi. How would the *gilgul* know the difference?

He put on his *tallit* and started to bless the girl, but the *gilgul* laughed.

'You're no rabbi! You're the one who caused all this in the first place!'

The carpenter was taken aback. 'Me? What did I do?'

'You cut down the tree I was sheltering in. Once I was a man. I died and there was no one to say *kaddish* [the mourning prayer] over my body. So instead of going straight to God's throne, my spirit remained, trapped. But I needed to be in a living being or I would have remained hovering over my grave forever, lost to both worlds. Luckily for me, a dog came scampering by. I entered his body with relief. I had a fine time searching for new smells, until a group of boys decided to tease me. They pelted me with stones and chased me into a meadow. The dog was lying broken and bleeding. I left it for the horse grazing nearby. I spent many years in the horse until one day it wandered into the forest and tripped over a rabbit hole. Before it died, I moved to a tree. That very tree you cut down! I had no choice. I had to enter your daughter's body.'

The *gilgul* stopped.

'I am so bored. I can't stand it in here. I just want this finished. Get me a rabbi!' The *gilgul* ended on a scream.

Well you can imagine the family's astonishment. After a quick consultation, the family sent a messenger for the rabbi.

The rabbi arrived. He listened to the family, he listened to the *gilgul*. The rabbi began to say *kaddish*. As he reached the last line, saying 'and let us say Amen,' there came an almighty shriek from the *gilgul*. 'At last!'

The family, and especially the daughter, were never troubled again.

LIVERPOOL

Liverpool Museum has an exhibition of the frontage of Galkoff's kosher butchers. On the back are reminiscences of Liverpool Jewry in the areas around Pembroke Place. Some remember the two red-headed butcher's boys cycling down each side of the river, others the smells and sights of living in such close quarters. The Liverpool Jewish community was initially transient … many were waiting for transport to America. But wherever there are people, there are goods to sell and needs to be met. Living in such crowded conditions, it was hard to keep clean. It was easier if your neighbour was Jewish too; no funny looks or remarks about the smells coming from your kitchen or why at certain times of the year there is more bustle than usual. One of these times is Passover. The house would be completely cleaned and all pockets turned out before the changing of the dishes from the *chometz* ones to the *pesachdik* ones. There is comfort in being part of a community. Traditional songs and stories were looked forward to, taught in *cheder*, told by grandparents to grandchildren, who then told parents busy with preparing for the festival.

This is a version of an ancient cumulative song sung at the very end of the *seder*, the meal on the first night of Passover.

Chad Gadya*

We lived in Pembroke Place, one of the last few courtyard housings in Liverpool. There were many families living cheek by jowl

---

* Ch pronounced like loch.

around us, from all over these islands and us from Poland. There
were as many Jews settled here as those waiting for transport to
America. Miss Auger, who cleaned and refurbished ostrich feathers, had her shop down the road and Mam cleaned there first thing
in the morning and again at the end of the day. Da tried for jobs
down the docks as and when they turned up. We lived around the
corner from Galkoff's kosher butchers. There were so many kosher
shops around but Galkoff's was the one near us.

Last night we searched the whole house with a candle and
feather, looking for the bits of stale bread Nomi, my elder sister,
had placed around, the last bits of *chometz*. This morning we burnt
them in the courtyard, in the bin the other Jews who lived in these
courts with us, placed theirs. We were so careful not to let the fire
get out of control. Mam set us, Hayim and me, to watch until the
bread was completely burnt. Then we came in and helped separate
the eggs, yolks in one bowl, whites in another. We cracked the nuts
and ground the almonds in the mortar, ready for both macaroons
and *charoset*, the mortar for the *seder*. Nomi had already taken out
the plates we used only this one week a year. I loved seeing the old
patterns again.

So we could have something hot to eat before the meal proper
we had boiled potatoes on big spoons to dip in salt water during the
seder. By the time the meal was finished and the *afikomen*, the last
piece of *matza*, found and eaten, we were half asleep. Father rushed
through the *benching* (saying grace) and *hallel* until we were onto the
songs and then we woke up, to sing, and shout our favourites.

This year I found the *afikomen* and father promised me something special. Now I was waiting to see what he would bring home.

I saw him coming down the lane with a piece of string in his
hand. There was a flash of white between his legs. I couldn't make
out what it was, until he was nearer. It was a baby goat, a kid!
A white kid!

'Is this for me, Da? Is the kid mine?' I was overjoyed and didn't
know who to embrace first, Da or the kid.

'I bought this white kid, this only kid, for two *zuzim* in the
market. Here you are.' He handed me the string.

I kissed his cheek and flung my arms around the kid. 'I love him already,' I said. 'I'll call him Chad Gadya, my only kid.'

'Be careful though,' said Da. 'He's very frail, that's why he was so cheap. Only two *zuzim*, that's all I paid for this kid.'

'I'll be careful,' I promised. 'I'll treasure him forever.'

I fed him and groomed him. I sang to him and played with him. I loved him.

Nomi and Hayim laughed at me. 'What do you want with that runt? It won't feed more than one of us.'

'My kid won't feed any of us,' I shouted. 'He's my kid, my only kid, that Da bought for two *zuzim*, Chad Gadya.'

One day a mangy cat ranged into the yard, looking for food. He was scrawny but street tough. I scared him off with a broom. I thought I had done enough to protect my kid, my only kid, Chad Gadya.

The cat crept back and attacked my kid. He killed him and sat there eating him as calm as could be when I found them. I cried and cried. The cat ate my kid, my only kid, that Da bought for two *zuzim*, Chad Gadya. I was inconsolable.

Nomi and Hayim helped to chase the cat away. It ran down the alley where the butcher's dog lay panting in the one pool of sunshine to reach our yard. It saw the cat running and lunged after it with a sharp bark. As the cat sped past, the dog opened his mouth and bit down hard. The cat screamed and leapt for the wall. The dog bit the cat that ate the kid that Da had bought for two *zuzim*, an only kid, my only kid, Chad Gadya.

I was glad. But the butcher came out of his shop. He rounded the corner away from his green-glazed tiles with their cream borders. 'I'll give you, barking like that! Disturbing my customers! Sha! Sha!' He raised his arm with a stick and brought it down on the dog. Whack!

'Oh no!' I cried. 'Don't hit the dog. He bit the cat that ate the kid that Da bought for two *zuzim*, an only kid, my only kid, Chad Gadya.'

The butcher shrugged, what did that matter? He had customers to serve. He wiped his hands down his striped apron and went back into the shop, dropping the stick in the pool of sunshine as he did so.

Hayim picked up the stick and ran it along the iron railings down the street. Near the old Zoological Gardens, it caught between the bars. Hayim pulled and pulled. The stick sizzled. A lick of fire spurted up. Hayim dropped the stick as it burst into flames. So fire burnt the stick that hit the dog that bit the cat that ate the kid that Da bought for two *zuzim*, the only kid, my only kid, Chad Gadya.

Luckily there was a water trough nearby and someone rushed out and grabbed the flaming stick from Hayim, throwing it into the trough and putting out the fire that burnt the stick that hit the dog that bit the cat that ate the kid that Da bought for two *zuzim*, an only kid, my only kid, Chad Gadya.

Hayim ran back to us, shouting all the while. Nomi and I couldn't believe it. We had to see the wet burnt stick for ourselves. It was floating in the water trough, black and wizened. Hayim poked it. It was still warm. Just then a cattle drover passed by with his herd. No one believes that Liverpool was surrounded by fields and it's only in the last fifty years that it was built up, so Mam told us.

The cows had walked in from the countryside and were so thirsty when they smelled water they crowded around the trough. We moved out of their way. We didn't want to be crushed. The cows drank up all the water that put out the fire that burnt the stick that hit the dog that bit the cat that ate the kid that Da bought for two *zuzim*, an only kid, my only kid, Chad Gadya.

The cows walked on to the ritual slaughterer who had a shed down by the docks. Hayim had seen the slaughterer sharpening his knife. A blessing and a quick stroke and it was over, so they said. The slaughterer slaughtered the cow that drank the water that put out the fire that burnt the stick that hit the dog that bit the cat that

ate the kid that Da bought for two *zuzim*, an only kid, my only kid, Chad Gadya.

It turned out that Reb Mottel, the ritual slaughterer, had a bad heart and not long after he collapsed at work and died. Mam said the Angel of Death had come and taken him. The Angel of Death killed the slaughterer who slaughtered the cow that drank the water that put out the fire that burnt the stick that hit the dog that bit the cat that ate the kid that Da bought for two *zuzim*, an only kid, my only kid, Chad Gadya.

In *cheder* we learnt the story of Passover, when the Angel of Death passed over the houses of the Children of Israel. 'Was there anything stronger than the Angel of Death?' we asked. 'Yes,' came the answer, 'the Holy One Blessed Be He. He can stop the Angel of Death and get rid of him.'

Along came the Holy One Blessed Be He who nullified the Angel of Death, who killed the slaughterer, who slaughtered the cow, that drank the water, that put out the fire, that burnt the stick, that hit the dog, that bit the cat, that ate the kid, that Da bought for two *zuzim*, an only kid, my only kid, Chad Gadya.

Every Jewish household that holds a *seder* on the first night of Passover will end up singing this cumulative song right at the end. The tunes vary, depending on family and custom. Some just chant the song, others try to sing it to a familiar melody; 'Waltzing Matilda' is one. It follows the path of songs like the 'House that Jack Built' but adds a serious note at the end. We are all, no matter who we are, subject to the Holy One Blessed Be He. Some say that the only kid was Israel, the Jews. This song has been traced back to Haggadot, books relating the story of the Exodus used at a *seder* table, of the thirteenth century. This is my translation from the *haggada*.

My father bought for two *zuzim* an only kid, an only kid.

A cat ate the kid that my father bought for two *zuzim*, an only kid, an only kid.

A dog bit the cat that ate the kid that my father bought for two *zuzim*, an only kid, an only kid.

A stick beat the dog that bit the cat that ate the kid my father bought for two *zuzim*, an only kid, an only kid.

Fire burnt the stick that beat the dog that bit the cat that ate the kid that my father bought for two *zuzim*, an only kid, an only kid.

Water quenched the fire that burnt the stick that beat the dog that bit the cat that ate the kid my father bought for two *zuzim*, an only kid, an only kid.

An ox drank the water that quenched the fire, that burnt the stick that beat the dog that bit the cat that ate the kid that my father bought for two *zuzim*, an only kid, an only kid.

The slaughterer killed the ox that drank the water that quenched the fire that burnt the stick that beat the dog that bit the cat that ate the kid my father bought for two *zuzim*, an only kid, an only kid.

The Angel of Death killed the slaughterer that killed the ox that drank the water that quenched the fire that burnt the stick that beat the dog that bit the cat that ate the kid that my father bought for two *zuzim*, an only kid, an only kid.

The Holy One Blessed Be He killed the Angel of Death that killed the slaughterer that killed the ox that drank the water that quenched the fire that burnt the stick that beat the dog that bit the cat that ate the kid that my father bought for two *zuzim*, an only kid, an only kid. Chad Gadya.

❧

With thirteen kosher butchers spread around Liverpool there were lots of chickens being plucked after ritual slaughter. Behind the buildings was a huge yard covered in clucking chickens. 'How many for Shabbos, Mrs Greenberg? Four? How about this one?' And the chicken man would hold up a luckless bird. 'Not big enough?' He put the bird down and delved into the flock, grabbing another. 'How about this one? Yes? Do you want it plucked too?' A nod and an extra ha'penny for the plucker. By the end of the day lots of chickens meant lots of feathers. Feathers also meant money. A poor man would come and buy the day's feathers from the yard. He would take them home to his back yard, where they would be washed and cleaned carefully before sorting, by the man, his wife and their children, coughing as they did so. The hard ones into this pile, the soft ones into that. Once sorted they would be sold by the weight for stuffing duvets and pillows, or for dyeing for hats and other decorations.

This favourite rabbinic story is set in Liverpool because of the preponderance of feathers.

FLYING FEATHERS

There was a problem for the Liverpool community. One of its outstanding businessmen couldn't resist embroidering the problems of his rivals, all to boost his own ego. It got so that in the end he had lucked on one poor individual who couldn't and wouldn't stand up to him in public. This opponent took all the rudeness and the exaggerated stories that the businessman threw at him, which of course made the man try to get some reaction from him.

Then, as these things happen, our businessman found out something awful but true about his rival. He couldn't resist. He went to *shul* in Princes Road that morning and passed on with a nod and a wink a little bit of the truth to the other men there. Men are such dreadful gossips, aren't they? The men rushed home to tell their wives. The wives met at the fishmongers and the bakers and one told another what they'd heard. Soon a version of the truth, worse than the actuality, had spread across Liverpool; even the Liver birds cawed about it.

The centre of this rumour finally heard it. This hit him in the heart and he couldn't believe a fellow Jew would say such a thing. He went to the rabbi and poured out his sorrows. The rabbi listened.

The next day the rabbi stopped our businessman as he was leaving the morning prayers. He blustered. 'But what's the problem, Rabbi? It's true, isn't it?'

'Whether it's true or not isn't the question,' answered the rabbi. 'What you've done is *lashon hara* [slander] and you've ruined his reputation. This is like murder.' The rabbi went on until the businessman not only understood what he'd done but felt sorry for it.

'How can I make it better?' he asked.

The rabbi looked at him. 'Do you have any feather pillows in your house?'

The businessman preened, 'Of course, plenty, with the best feathers, the softest grade. How many do you want?'

'Just the one. Bring it to me this afternoon. We'll meet upstairs in the Women's Gallery.'

That afternoon the businessman brought his whitest, softest pillow to the rabbi. They climbed the stairs to the Women's Gallery. The pair looked down at the *shul* from this unusual angle. They saw what the women saw as they sat listening and watching the service taking place so far below them. They saw the pillars rising high above them to make the graceful arches, the clear rose window over the beautiful blue domes with their gold stars and Hebrew inscription that honoured the *aron hakodesh*, the Holy Ark that contained the *Sifrei Torah*, the Torah Scrolls. They looked down on the *bimah*, the reading desk where the *chazan* stood to lead the prayers, the pews with their wooden arms and leather box seats on either side under the Women's Gallery. The *shul* was gorgeous, ornate, intricate.

The rabbi looked the pillow over and nodded. He handed the businessman a knife.

'Cut it,' he said.

'What?'

'Cut it,' repeated the rabbi.

Mystified, the businessman cut the pillow open.

'Now, shake the feathers out,' said the rabbi.

'Well if that's what you want!'

And the businessman shook the pillow with all his strength.

The feathers flew out and gusted round the *shul*. They whirled up to the ceiling and floated down among the lights, trapping in the chains before drifting off to fall here, there and everywhere. A slight draught from the doors upstairs and downstairs caught some and hustled them out into the busy world of Princes Road.

The rabbi looked at the blanket of feathers. The businessman looked at the blanket of feathers. A few minutes later, as feathers fell off the *ner tamid*, the Eternal Light hung in front of the *aron hakodesh*, to the floor, the rabbi spoke again.

'Now collect them all up and bring them back. All, mind, every single one of them.'

'But that's impossible, Rabbi. I'll never get them all. Some will have gone down the cracks in the seats, others behind the domes. And I know some went out into the street.'

'Yes,' nodded the rabbi, 'that's how it's done with a rumour, one of your stories, a little gossip here and there. You don't know where it goes and you can never call it back.'

The businessman realised what he'd really done. The rabbi made him apologise and compensate the man he'd wronged. He had to apologise to all the people he'd shared the story with, too. He never exaggerated again, nor told stories about other people. And the whole congregation were reminded to watch what they said as well on the occasional Shabbos when they saw a feather floating above their heads, coming from, it seemed, the very heavens.

During the story collecting in Liverpool the topic of how Liverpool Jews managed during the war came up. A number of Kindertransport children were taken in by the Liverpool community just before the war. A member of our group remembered one child, a little girl of 6, who came to live with her family. The girl couldn't speak any English and it took a couple of days before the host family found a silver plate sewn into the lining of her coat. She couldn't tell the family anything about herself but she could remember this song, 'Az der rebbe tantst'. The daughter of the family filled with tears as we who had listened to her story, sang the song she hadn't heard since then, with her.

AZ DER REBBE TANTST

When the Rabbi dances, oh when the Rabbi dances, dance all
the Hasidim, when the Rabbi dances, oh when the Rabbi dances,
dance all the Hasidim.

When the Rabbi sings, oh when the Rabbi sings, sing all the
Hasidim, when the Rabbi sings, oh when the Rabbi sings, sing all
the Hasidim.

When the Rabbi drinks, oh when the Rabbi drinks, drink all the
Hasidim, when the Rabbi drinks, oh when the Rabbi drinks, drink
all the Hasidim.

When the Rabbi laughs, oh when the Rabbi laughs, laugh all the
Hasidim, when the Rabbi laughs, oh when the Rabbi laughs, laugh
all the Hasidim.

When the Rabbi sleeps, oh when the Rabbi sleeps, sleep all the
Hasidim, when the Rabbi sleeps, oh when the Rabbi sleeps, sleep
all the Hasidim.

MANCHESTER

Rabbi Shacter was known as the penny *rav*. Ask him a *shayla*, a religious question, and it would only cost you one penny. The difficulty is, ask a question and you have to abide by the answer. Many a time he had to answer a *shayla* about a bloodspot in an egg, or a blemish on the inside of a chicken from the many women who lived in the crowded conditions in central Manchester. And many an egg was poured down the drain.

During our story-collecting session in Heathlands Village, Manchester, one woman recalled how as a child she had to carry the live chicken to the *shochet* in a basket. She then had to carry the dead chicken back home. On the way there she was scared the chicken would poke its head out and peck her; on the way back she was scared the dead chicken would come to life again!

Another woman remembered that going to the *mikveh* behind the English *shul* in Cheetham Hill was better than the old square tub with step down and cold water in Hay Lane. Even if you came out with a wet head and all the yobs wondered why you went swimming at night.

An elderly man in Manchester calls his son in London and says, 'I hate to ruin your day, but I have to tell you that your mother and I are divorcing. Forty-five years of misery is enough.'

'Dad, what are you talking about?' the son screams.

'We can't stand the sight of each other any longer,' the old man says. 'We're sick of each other, and I'm sick of talking about this, so you call your sister in Glasgow and tell her,' and he hangs up.

Frantic, the son calls his sister, who explodes on the phone. 'This is not going to happen,' she shouts, 'I'll make sure of it.'

She calls her father immediately and screams at the old man, 'You are NOT getting divorced! Don't do a single thing until I get there. I'm calling my brother back, and we'll both be there tomorrow. Until then, don't do a thing, DO YOU HEAR ME?' and hangs up.

The old man hangs up his phone and turns to his wife. 'OK,' he says, 'they're coming for Passover and paying their own fares.'

The Sephardi community, coming from Aleppo, Cairo, Syria and Gibraltar, soon established their own synagogue after using the old Jews' School on Cheetham Hill Road. Their architect, Edward Salomon, created a building in the style of medieval Spain on the same street. It is now the Jewish Museum, retaining the original synagogue in all its Sephardic splendour and colour. In the coffee shops the community loved so much, stories were swapped as well as deals made and tobacco smoked. They flourished in Manchester, bringing more prosperity to the city and adding Ladino (Judaeo–Spanish) to the language mix. This story begins with a yearning song in Ladino, and is based on a famous Spanish ballad that the Sephardi Jews were known to have taken with them when they were expelled in 1492, keeping it alive in the language of the time in the lands they found themselves in, and eventually ending up in Britain.

THE JEALOUS QUEEN

Durme, durme, mi alma donzella	Sleep, sleep, my beloved damsel
durme, durme, sin ansia y dolor	sleep, sleep, without anxiety or pain
durme, durme, sin ansia y dolor.	sleep, sleep, without anxiety or pain.
Que tu sclavo que tanto desea	Here is your slave who so wants
ver tu sueño con grande amor	to watch over your dreams with the greatest love
ver tu sueño con grande amor.	to watch over your dreams with the greatest love.

Dur-me,dur - me mi - al-ma do-n ze-lla dur-me, dur-me sin - an-sia y do - lor dur - me

dur - me sin an - sia y do - lor.

Every night the princess could hear this song but no matter how hard she looked out into the dark night she couldn't see the singer who serenaded her.

The moon shone on the lake beneath the castle windows and she thought she caught a glimpse of a head in the black waters, but she wasn't sure. She wondered, 'Is that him?'

The servants gossiped and talked of a merman in the lake, singing to bring his true love to him. The queen dismissed the idea of a merman but secretly she hoped for it. The princess smiled to herself and kept her own counsel.

That night the queen stayed up late. She was sewing a gown for the ball in honour of her daughter's 16th birthday. Now everyone knows that a queen has plenty of people to sew gowns for her but it seemed that whatever they brought her wasn't good enough and the only way she knew to get things done as she wanted was … to do it herself.

So that night she was sewing away, her needle stabbing in and out, thinking of all the things she could have done to that fool of a seamstress who had tried to show her a dress fit for a dowager, not the vibrant, voluptuous woman she was. She thought of Count

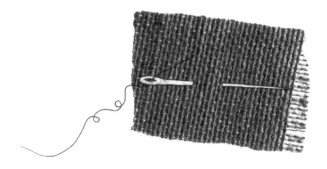

Olinos, her neighbour, a younger man to be sure, but now she was a widow, well … a queen can look at anybody.

As her needle attacked the fabric, she heard through her open window a singer, a singer with a sweet voice singing '*Durme, durme, mi alma donzella*'. She didn't wait to hear more. She threw down her sewing and ran down the corridor to her daughter's bedroom.

'I heard the merman singing to me tonight. Did you hear him too?'

'I heard Count Olinos singing, Mama, singing of his love for me.' Her daughter looked straight at her mother.

Her mother took a step backwards. 'No! It was the merman! And he sang for me, for me, not you!'

'It is Olinos, Mama,' the princess insisted. 'He sings every night. He loves me. I love him. We are just waiting for my sixteenth birthday. And … of course … your permission.' Her daughter lowered her eyes.

'That you will never have!' spat her mother. 'Nor Olinos. You will never marry.'

The queen turned on her heel and went back to her room to tear the tiny stitches out of her dress. She ordered the arrest of Count Olinos. 'Let him rot in jail, for all I care,' she sobbed.

Count Olinos was made of stern stuff. He stayed true to his love for the princess and refused the queen. She was incensed and ordered his execution. She insisted that the princess watch him die.

As the shots rang out and Olinos' body hit the ground, the princess's heart broke. She died a moment after him. The queen ordered them to be buried, in separate graves far apart. That was the end of the matter as far as she was concerned; she would grieve in private.

After some while the servants' gossip reached the queen's ears. She strode out to the graves to see for herself. From Olinos' grave, a flowering honeysuckle grew and stretched and crept to the princess' grave, where a rambling rose grew and stretched until the two bushes intertwined and could not be separated.

In a rage the queen ordered the gardeners to grub up both bushes and throw them on a bonfire. The released petals floated up in the smoke to be carried higher by the wind. They turned into birds, he a hawk, she a dove. The hawk sheltered the dove in his wings as they flew up into the sky.

'Quickly!' ordered the queen, 'Shoot them down!'

The soldiers did not miss and the two birds plummeted towards the ground. They hit the waters of the lake that surrounded the castle. Under the water the two turned to fish. He to a salmon, she to a carp. The queen had the lake dragged until the fish were caught.

The bones of the fish were ground into dust and buried under the queen's doorstep.

The lovers changed one last time, he to a scorpion, she to a snake.

When the queen walked out of her castle the scorpion bit her. And so she died, the biter bit.

As Manchester Jews became more affluent, they moved out to the suburbs of Whitefields and Prestwich. Heaton Park was a favourite place for families to go to on Shabbos. English was heard more than Yiddish. Men wore hats and the boys patterned knitted skullcaps, *kipot*. Women wore hats or even went bareheaded. Now the younger section of the community tends to be ultra-Orthodox. Wonderful *sheitls* (wigs) or headscarves to cover the married women's hair abound. Girls wear long skirts but the knitted *kipot* or bare heads of the men are few and far between, instead there is a sea of black hats. Yiddish has had a resurgence. They still promenade through Heaton Park on Shabbos. Families are large, as are the cars that crowd and double park during the week. The grocery shops are full with items carrying kosher certification and pop-up shops appear before each religious festival selling everything you could need.

I found this story in the Israel Folklore Archive, University Haifa.

REACHING FOR RIGHTS

We meet in Rochele's house, every Wednesday afternoon. There's always a discussion on the week's *sedra*. We take this very seriously because didn't Rabbi Eliezar say, 'One who teaches his daughter [Oral] Torah – it is as though he teaches her frivolity.'*

We don't want to be accused of frivolity or anything that smacks of inattention in our learning. We want equal status in Judaism. We want to be called up to the Torah in the *shul* alongside men. We want to lay *tefillin* bands on our arms and as a sign between our eyes every morning. We want to stand like the Women of the Wall and pray at our holiest site with equal rights in our prayer shawls. We want to be rabbis, not *rebbetzins*, the wives of rabbis. And we want to do it as Orthodox women.

We talk about this every week. And every week we get more militant. Why not? Who's to stop us? Whom should we ask the question? For if we ask a question of a rabbi then we have to abide by the answer. Now that's fine when we're not sure whether what we can see in the glass is a bloodspot or not; is it in the yolk or the white. Does it matter as long as we don't eat blood, right? Right.

But on women's rights, should a rabbi, a man, rule? We argue and argue. Until someone, I don't know who, says, 'Well the only one who can rule on this is God. Why don't we ask God?'

---

* Babylonian Talmud. Sota 20a.

Now this starts another argument over whether our prayers aren't asking God all the time. But Rochele says the only way to settle the problem once and for all is to go and speak to God face to face, like Moses did. 'One of us should go up to heaven and put our point of view directly to HaShem. I'm certain we'll succeed.'

After a minute or so of absolute silence, something that is so rare as to be appreciated, an argument breaks out over who should go.

'She needs to be someone who speaks and doesn't shout,' says Malka, looking pointedly at Shura. Poor Shura finds it impossible to speak in a quiet tone. Even her whispers are loud.

Shura takes this on the chin and says, 'Well, she must be learned.' This makes Malka mad, she's oversensitive about her struggle to understand the finer points. She's still at the basic level.

It goes on and on. Until someone, I don't know who, shouts 'Shah!' and we all shut up.

Rivka, our oldest member, staggers to her feet and that is hard for her with her legs these days.

'It's obvious!' she says.

We look at each other; so why are we arguing if it's so obvious? Rivka shakes her head at our ignorance.

'Shprintzel* should go,' she declaims in a quavery voice.

And at once it's indisputable. Shprintzel should go. Someone, I don't know who, says she'll tell her when she sees her at the women-only swimming session on Thursday morning. A committee forms to help Shprintzel prepare her petition.

We all sigh and reach for the cake Rochele has baked specially for our meetings.

When we meet the following Wednesday, we find we have a problem. Shprintzel agrees to go and is preparing her speech. But she asks how is she going to meet God?

We look up the sources and come to the conclusion that God is in heaven and that is above the sky. We read the story of the Tower of Babel and how close it came to breaching heaven.

---

* Shprintzel, a Yiddish girl's name meaning Hope.

Someone, I don't know who, suggests we should make a tower and reach the moon and from there Shprintzel could stretch up and get into heaven that way.

'A tower? A tower of what? We don't have anything to build a tower with.' And before another argument can start, Rivka stops us with one shaking hand.

'We have our bodies.'

At once it is obvious.

We agree to gather as many women as possible and meet in Heaton Park, in the largest open space we could find. We would do it the next new moon as it's auspicious in two ways: one is that as it's the women's monthly festival, our men wouldn't expect us to do any work for them. The second is that as it is a crescent moon, Shprintzel would find it easier to grab hold and haul herself up before launching herself into heaven.

So here we are in Heaton Park. At least it's not raining. Not today. It did yesterday. Luckily, we have thought about that and have brought blankets. We spread them out over the grass and wait for all the women to arrive. They start coming at twilight.

They come in their hundreds. We are astonished. This is what social media does for you. All ages and all determined to get the answer from God. We all want equality, don't we?

Rochele organises us. The older ones with their zimmer frames form the base of the tower. Each woman climbs up on the back of the woman below and bends over so the next layer can climb up. It takes a very long time. The sky is dark now. The tower grows higher and higher. It reaches above the trees, it reaches up to the clouds, it reaches beyond.

Someone, I don't know who, calls down for Shprintzel to begin her ascent, as Moses did on Mount Sinai. The moon appears bright and sharp, just above.

Shprintzel climbs up the tower of women and gets to the top. She stretches up, her fingertips graze the tip of the crescent. She reaches up.

Down at the bottom of the tower the elderly women are in trouble. They have been standing with their backs bent for many

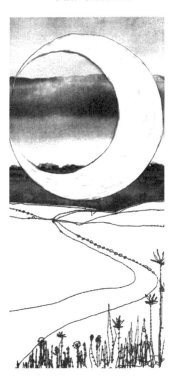

hours. They all want to go to the toilet. Then someone, I don't know who, screams their leg is in spasm. She can't control it.

The tower shakes.

The tower leans.

The tower falls.

When all the ambulances have been and gone and we have a list of who is in hospital, we check everyone else.

One is missing.

It's Shprintzel.

She's made it. She's in heaven talking to God.

So now when we meet on a Wednesday, we all call out as we enter Rochele's house, 'Has Shprintzel come yet?'

We are waiting for her to return and give us God's answer. We are waiting for equality.

BIRMINGHAM

The city of a thousand trades drew many Jews in the early 1700s. They were pedlars, watchmakers, optical glass grinders and jewellers. Mention was made at the time of the fried fish that the Jews in Birmingham loved so much. The first synagogue was in the Froggery area of Birmingham although this was later bombed and redeveloped. The community thrived, the pedlars evolving into shopkeepers, their children going to school, learning English and other secular subjects. A Jewish school was founded and the Singers Hill Synagogue built. They became prosperous.

This is a tale from the Talmud about cleverness and greed.

FOUR BOILED EGGS

Zisl lifted his pack one more time onto his shoulder. He was tired. He had been walking for a long time. He was hungry and still had miles to go before he got to Birmingham. He hoped that there was an inn over the brow of the hill. This part of Warwickshire was gently undulating but straining on the legs.

Thankfully he saw an inn on the Hagley Road. He went in and asked for a meal. As he was Jewish, he couldn't eat the usual fare on offer, but the innkeeper's wife boiled four eggs for him. He wolfed them down, grateful to fill his belly. The innkeeper charged him sixpence for the four eggs. Zisl nodded. He looked for his coin purse. It had gone. He saw the frayed string that had tied it to his pack. He explained the problem to the innkeeper and promised to return and pay him. The innkeeper nodded. He understood all right.

Zisl walked on, weighed down both by the loss of his purse and the coin inside and the debt to the innkeeper. He was saddened by both. He was determined to stay in one place in future and have a shop. That way this kind of accidental loss could never happen to him again.

In Birmingham, Zisl worked hard, first at one of the many Jewish fish and chip shops that had sprung up. Then, when he had gathered a bit of money, he started his own business, selling pens and the pen nibs that were made locally. He and Birmingham prospered. He married a clever woman who helped him in growing his business and his family grew, too. He was happy. Except that every now and then he remembered his debt to the innkeeper on the Hagley Road, it was just that he worked every day except Shabbat. And he wouldn't break Shabbat.

One Friday he had an unexpected day off. The first thing he did was to ride up to the inn on the Hagley Road. The same innkeeper was at the bar. His wife was cleaning the tables. They both stared when the well-dressed customer walked in.

Zisl went up to the bar and said he wanted to settle his bill.

'And what bill is that, sir?' asked the innkeeper, not recognising him.

'Several years ago, you gave me a meal of four boiled eggs. I couldn't pay you because I had lost my purse. I've come to settle up with you now.'

The innkeeper understood. He looked at this well-dressed man in front of him. He remembered the pedlar he'd been before.

'Let's see,' he said, licking a stub of pencil. 'I have to work this out. Four eggs at sixpence, now they could've hatched a chicken each, those chickens could've laid sixteen eggs each. I make that sixty-four. They would have hatched 1,024 chickens. Those chickens would have hatched 16,384 …'

The innkeeper continued calculating until he finally said, 'I make it you owe me £39,321 and six shillings.'

'What!' exclaimed Zisl. 'How can that be? I don't have such a large amount, not on me, not in the bank.'

'Unless you pay me, I'll have the law on you. I know who you are now,' sneered the innkeeper.

Zisl went home slowly. He sat down heavily at the Shabbat table. His wife and children gathered round, they had never seen Zisl so shattered.

He told his wife the story. She listened carefully and then patted him on the shoulder. 'Make the blessing over the wine and *challot*. I have a solution.'

Zisl brightened up. Marrying his wife was the best thing he had ever done. He knew he could rely on her. The Shabbat meal had never tasted so sweet.

On Sunday morning, Zisl and his wife and children all rode up the Hagley Road to the inn. The innkeeper came swaggering out.

'Have you brought my money? I got your note and the local magistrate is in the bar to see fair play.'

'Good,' said Zisl's wife and she swept past with the children, leaving the innkeeper open-mouthed in her wake.

In the bar, the local magistrate was partaking of the local brew. He wiped his moustache when he saw the woman and children enter.

'Here, here, my good woman, what is all this?'

Zisl's wife lifted up the basket she carried. 'I've come to plant the corn in the field behind the inn.'

'Really? First I've heard of it,' said the magistrate. 'I didn't know it was going to be planted. Let's have a look at this corn of yours.'

He lifted the lid of the basket and guffawed. 'This is cooked corn. You're not going to get much corn from this. Boiled corn won't grow.'

'Neither,' said Zisl's wife, 'can boiled eggs hatch!'

The magistrate had to agree and dismissed the innkeeper's claim completely. He also insisted on another pint on the house for troubling him. Zisl paid the innkeeper's wife sixpence for the four eggs and another nine shillings and sixpence for the wait. She was more than contented.

Zisl, his wife and children rode back to Birmingham, happy once more.

The magistrate let it be known about the innkeeper's greed and calculations. He became a laughing stock. He had to turn the business over to his wife, who kept a strict eye on him and the takings.

Birmingham has a varied community, running from the ultra-Orthodox Lubavitch, through modern Orthodox, Masorti, Reform, Progressive and non-affiliated. There are three synagogues in Birmingham itself, the Liberal and Progressive with a female rabbi, and another Orthodox in nearby Solihull. The Jewish primary school attracts more non-Jewish pupils than Jewish.

There is a high number of academics due to the Birmingham universities and those in nearby Keele in one direction and Oxford in the other. It has a vibrant Jewish student society due to outreach Student Chaplain Rabbi Fishel Cohen and his wife, Esther.

This is a true story.

TEFILLIN AND MEZUZOT

A synagogue used to be on Park Road, Moseley, until the late 1990s. It is now a Buddhist centre. Orthodox Jews tend to live within walking distance of their synagogue, so it's not surprising to find Jews living around the environs of the old *shul* and Moseley Park. As Britain's second city, Birmingham has its fair share of crime. A Jewish house on Park Road was targeted by local thieves. In the space of six months the house had been broken into three times. Each time the thieves waited for the insurance to pay out and new objects to be bought.

Despite the fact there was a burglar alarm and security locks on the windows, the family couldn't work out why they were targeted, especially after the first time. They had lost jewellery, which was sentimental rather than precious, and camera equipment, but then their home didn't contain much in the way of pickings or *tchatchkes* (small ornaments). This family had a house filled … with books and children.

The mother arrived home with the children one day after school to find the chain on the door on the inside. She raced around the side fence but was too late. The thieves had bolted with, among other things, her engagement ring, earrings and a couple of family pocket watches.

One surprising item stolen was the husband's *tefillin* bag, with his *tefillin* in. *Tefillin* are phylacteries, two boxes with leather straps, containing four handwritten scrolls where *tefillin* are mentioned in the Torah, twice in Exodus and twice in Deuteronomy. Men 'lay *tefillin*', put them on, during the morning prayers, *shakharit*, wrapping the straps around the right arm with one box facing into the heart and the rest of the straps wound around the arm and then fingers. The other box is placed on the forehead with the box above and between the eyes, the straps hanging down the back. As these are regarded as holy, they are usually kept inside an embroidered velvet bag.

Obviously, the thieves thought the velvet bag contained valuable items. What else but jewellery would be in an embroidered velvet bag? Imagine their dismay when they opened the bag to find leather straps and black wooden boxes! The police were bemused to find the velvet bag thrown on the ground near the back fence. The *tefillin* were still inside. Not worth anything to thieves but so much to the family.

The community commiserated. The family were visited by the rabbis of the community, including the Lubavitcher rabbonim. One of them was a *sofer* (a scribe). He asked the family if they'd ever had their *mezuzot* checked. Like the *tefillin*, the *mezuzah* contains the passages of the Shema, Judaism's central statement of the oneness of God. It is written in the book of Exodus in the Torah.

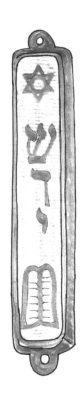

Most Jewish houses have a *mezuzah* on the front doorpost on the right-hand side in the top third as you face the door. Inside the house, some have a *mezuzah* on every door except the bathroom and toilet. The cases can vary from the plain to the ornate, from wood to ceramic or silver, from the tiny to the elongated. They are the armour for the *klaf*, the paper inside. This is a sliver of parchment with handwritten paragraphs of the Shema and then rolled up to fit inside the case. Sometimes the cost of the *klaf* was double or triple the cost of the case. Putting up a *mezuzah* on the house is fulfilling the Torah commandment to put it on the doorpost of your house. Some people kiss the case with their fingertips every time they enter or leave as added holiness. A *mezuzah* means protection to most Jews. They see it as having God's presence over their house. Even if they don't believe, they feel that it holds power. Often they forget what is written on the internal scroll, they just understand it means they are guarded from evil.

The family had brought their *mezuzot* with them from Israel. They were the first things they attached when they took possession of the house. Now the rabbi was saying there was something wrong with their *mezuzot*. The family was filled with dread. He offered to check them for any problems.

A family, he said, had a child who was constantly falling ill. The doctors couldn't find a cause, but the family had their *mezuzot* checked by a local *sofer*. He found there was a mistake in the one on the door to the child's room. When this was replaced the child improved and soon was back to full health.

'From this we have to have our *mezuzot* examined?' asked the mother.

'Yes,' replied the *sofer*, 'the paper could have deteriorated and rubbed out some words.' He went on, 'You know, your *tefillin* were thrown back because they were kosher.'

The family understood that meant God was protecting the *tefillin*. But even so, could the *sofer* be right? Could the *mezuzot* be faulty and the cause of their problems?

It took until the third robbery before the family were convinced. Then they had all the *mezuzot* in the house checked. The front door *mezuzah* was in a glass tube secured by wooden ends. One of the children had made the ends in school. Unfortunately, rain had got in and in a couple of places the words had been washed away. The *sofer* made adjustments and repairs and soon had the *klafim* back inside their cases, with a new case for the front door. The family breathed a sigh of relief. They were safe again.

That very week, a couple of likely lads burgled a neighbour's house without realising he was asleep downstairs in his chair. He chased the boys out onto the road and sat on one's back until the police arrived. The boys owned up to the whole slew of robberies in Park Road and St George's Road. The house wasn't troubled by robbery again. The family all kissed the *mezuzah* as they entered and left though, just to be sure.

❦

What's more, in another city the Jewish houses all had *mezuzot* and they were free from crime. Another faith leader asked the local rabbi why this was so as his neighbourhood was plagued by robberies. The rabbi said it was because the *mezuzah* offered God's protection. 'Wonderful,' said the faith leader, 'where can I get them?' 'Here,' said the rabbi, handing him a bag of *mezuzot*, 'have these.'

A couple of months after the faith leader returned and thrust the bag of *mezuzot* into the hands of the rabbi. 'Have them back!' he exclaimed.

The rabbi was astonished. 'They didn't work?'

'Ha!' said the faith leader. 'True we have no more robberies …'

'So …' encouraged the rabbi.

'Now we have fundraisers!'

Swansea

The Swansea Jewish community is the oldest in Wales and one of the oldest in Britain. Known Jews were living in Swansea according to a Lodge census in 1725. Certainly by 1730 there was an established community who bought a plot of land in 1768 to bury their congregants. David Michael, the silversmith, had arrived in 1749 from Germany and was the instigator of the purchase. He undertook to pay the Burgesses ten shillings a year in rent plus a couple of fat pullets to the Portreeve or Mayor. His house was used for prayers with an extension on the back. Swansea flourished and so did the Jewish community. The third *shul* to be built was in Goat Street. After a series of accidents and war, eighty years later the community had to rebuild elsewhere. There were whispers the *shul* was cursed. Here is the story.

The Shul with Tzores

Swansea Jewish community was flourishing. David Michael's *shtiebl* extension had served its purpose and its successor was now bursting at the seams. The congregants needed a new synagogue. They tried to raise the money among themselves, but fell short of the total needed. Someone suggested they write to the *Jewish Chronicle* and appeal to the whole of Jewish Britain for help. After all, Swansea held an historic position in the story of British Jews, they were bound to help. Wasn't it one of the rabbis' sayings that one should help to build synagogues, ritual baths and schools? They'd forgotten that buying a cemetery was part of that saying, too.

Not only was the letter published but the *Jewish Chronicle* decided to support the appeal themselves. In no time the plot was purchased on Goat Street and the building erected. The committee were pleased and wrote to the Chief Rabbi, Nathan Adler, to preside over the consecration. He accepted with pleasure.

The day drew near. The Ladies Guild was kept busy making sandwiches and cakes for the celebration tea after the ceremony. They arranged bowls of chopped herring, egg and onion and, most extravagant of all, cod's roe – kosher caviar – with crackers. They put out the china cups and saucers, each with their own teaspoon, in rows in front of the huge metal teapots. There were bowls ready for the washing of hands, with jugs of water and folded towels on a table in the corner of the hall. They could do no more. The *gabbai* (treasurer) of the *shul* was sent to meet the train, the Chief Rabbi and a reporter.

The men gathered in the new synagogue. The President of the *shul* wore his best top hat, the other men their best hats and stiff collars. The women leaned over the railings of the Ladies Gallery to catch a glimpse of the Chief Rabbi when he came. Their hats vied with each other for the best view. There was a whisper, then a mutter. Movement at the doorway signified the arrival of the special guest. The men moved into their new seats ready for *mincha*, the afternoon service, to begin. The *gabbai* ushered in a young man to the seat of honour beside the *aron hakodesh*.

'That's the Chief Rabbi,' exclaimed one of the women, 'he's younger than my hat! I thought he was an old man.' The women whispered back and fore. Some tried to catch the eyes of their husbands below and ask a wordless question. The answer was given by the lad himself.

He stood on the *bimah* and took hold of the lectern. He gave his father's apologies. Rabbi Nathan Adler was too ill to attend but had sent his son, Hermann, in his place. Newly ordained Hermann gave his very first sermon and blessed the *shul*. Who knows, perhaps thinking it would be getting the weighty blessing of the Chief Rabbi and getting instead the light blessing of the son, no matter how sincere, wasn't good enough for the building.

From then on there was nothing but strife between the members. Where before they had talked then argued things out, now it went from arguments to *broygus*, where they wouldn't do a good turn for someone they thought had wronged them.

Someone said a *kelalah* (a curse) had been placed on the *shul*. The *sedra* of the blessings and the curses in Deuteronomy had been read out loud instead of whispering them as custom dictated from medieval times. Quarrels arose out of nowhere, petty arguments spilled out causing great hurt. One member wanted to put a head-stone on his late wife's grave. He arrived at the cemetery with the stone to find the gates locked against him. The officials wouldn't let him in because of a disagreement about his members' fees. Two other members turned up with their stones. They were refused entry as well in case by opening the gates for them, the first man would slip through.

Letters were written to the *Jewish Chronicle* about the high cost of wedding fees. Instead of keeping their dirty linen in-house and in Swansea, the congregants seemed determined to let everyone know what was going on. Arguments broke out over who should take the services. Mr Goldberg insisted that it was his and only his privilege. Members didn't like the way Mr Goldberg led them. Who was he anyway? He wasn't a rabbi or even a reverend. And if he could take the services then so could anyone else. Aspersions were cast on his *kashrut* and whether he kept Shabbat properly. Feelings escalated, tempers rose, no service was conducted in decorum as shouting frequently broke out in the *shul*. The letters asserted that spikes had been placed on the seats of the synagogue. A visit from Chief Rabbi Adler was necessary. The son, this time, not the father.

The weight of his office added to his merit and had the power to settle matters both for the building and the congregants. From now on the prayers and services would follow the '*Minhag* Poland', the custom of Polish Jews as well as the Chief Rabbi's office. And most importantly, Mr Goldberg would continue as the *Baltefila* (Reader) and *Baltekea* (blower of the ram's horn) 'on every occasion as long as he thinks fit and when he decides to discontinue same no other private member be allowed to act as *Baltefila* and *Baltekea*.' Mutterings followed but they had to obey the Chief Rabbi.

The influx of poorer Jews from Eastern Europe upset the balance once again. The Goat Street building felt slighted by their objections. The services were too establishment, too lax in observances. These Jews didn't like the way they were run. They broke away to form another congregation. Somehow Goat Street Synagogue prevailed and the breakaways slunk back. They were subsumed into the congregation. Perhaps that had been enough for the curse. Things quietened down for a while. Quiet didn't mean there were no arguments, just that they managed to keep them to themselves and didn't broadcast them in the *Jewish Chronicle*.

For its fiftieth anniversary Chief Rabbi Hermann Adler returned for a three-day fest that caused the *gabbai* to resign; Rabbi Adler expected so much and the *shul* couldn't pay for it all. When he died, Swansea sighed in relief. They hoped the curse had died with him.

They were wrong.

Three years later a fire broke out in the synagogue, destroying the schoolrooms. New premises for the children, a *mikveh* and a poultry yard, were found. But the synagogue couldn't keep its officials for long. They appointed Rev. S.J. Goldberg from Grimsby as minister. He was not popular and loved arguing. The sick building made him worse. No one would work with him. Soon there was a steady stream of men for the joint positions of *chazan/shochet/ mohel** arriving and then leaving. One didn't even bother to turn up after agreeing to come by letter. Instead he sent his brother and he only lasted a year.

Rev. H. Fineberg of Kalisz, Poland, arrived on a fresh wind with the taste of salt in his beard. Maybe the building had an inkling he would stay and tried to get rid of him. The first Yom Kippur service he took went off with a bang. The Nag's Head Inn next door had a gas leak and blew up, causing massive damage and injuries to the crowded synagogue.

---

* Leader of the services (singer)/ritual slaughterer/ritual circumciser.

⁓

Despite Rev. Fineberg being commended for his courage in carrying on with the service, the synagogue committee wobbled. Should they keep him or not? One vote carried the day and he stayed.

Rev. Goldberg stormed off. The situation was vacant for a long time. The building smouldered. It took Rev. Weintrobe, newly ordained from Jews College in London, to calm things down. He had no axe to grind, no other congregation with which to compare Goat Street. In 1941 he was released by the *shul* committee into the Chaplaincy of HM Forces. A month after he left, Goat Street Synagogue was hit by a German bomb and destroyed.

Not surprisingly, the Swansea Jewish community rebuilt elsewhere.

In the great movement of Jews from the Russian empire from the 1870s onward, many arrived in Britain, landing first in London's East End then moving out west in search of a better life. As so often happened, family members started on the road together only to split up, all the better to earn a living. Some went south-west to Exeter, Plymouth and Cornwall, some went west to Bristol and the communities of Wales. Life became just like the folk tales told of far-off times; a struggle to live, a struggle to keep Shabbos, a hope that things will get better, with the help of God something will turn up.

Joseph Only-the-Best-for-Shabbos

Joseph worked hard six days a week to provide the best for Shabbos. His neighbours mocked him. Only the best for Shabbos, only the best for Shabbos. He bought the best fish for Friday night at the market. When his wife lit the Shabbos candles, peace descended on Joseph's house. He did no work until after he had lit the Havdalah candle, smelled the spices and drunk the wine the following night. His wife prepared all the food beforehand so she too could rest. The family spent the day in prayer and song, honouring Shabbos.

A wealthy man saw how Joseph struggled each week to buy the best for Shabbos. He was angered by a prediction that all his wealth would go to Joseph on his death. He couldn't allow that. All his wealth in the hands of someone who scraped barely enough to eat each week? And that person Joseph 'Only-the-Best-for-Shabbos'? It wasn't to be borne. He had to find a way around his fate.

He sold up all his businesses and put the money into a precious jewel. This jewel he sewed into his hat and sailed away for foreign shores. Whilst on board ship, a huge storm came up. The hat was torn from the wealthy man's head by a strong gust of wind. It flew off across the ocean. The man screamed for the loss of his treasure; his words drowned by the wind.

On Friday, Joseph went down to the fish market. He jingled coins in his bag. He had more than usual and was on the lookout for the best fish for Shabbos. He spotted an unusually large fish and bought it.

He struggled to get it home and then gutted it and scaled it so his wife could cook it. From the innards, Joseph pulled a huge jewel. He couldn't believe his eyes. He called his wife. They stared at the jewel with glistening eyes. Their struggles were over.

The following week, Joseph bought the best fish for Shabbos he could. He held his house open to all the Jews in the area who wanted or needed to share a Shabbos meal. The evening was full of song and praise for God and Shabbos. From then on, all the poor were welcome to share his Shabbos meals.

Only the best for Shabbos.

CARDIFF

Cardiff, on the mouth of the Taff, has a wonderful fish market. Jews patronise the stalls knowing that the white fish they love – hake, cod, haddock, whiting, pollack (not to mention the Jewish favourite for *simchas* (celebrations) salmon), are in plentiful supply on Thursdays and Fridays. Fish holds so much symbolism in Judaism. A traditional dish served on *Rosh HaShonnah* (New Year), specifically the head of the fish, representing the head of the year, is offered to the head of the household first. No wonder that so many tales include treasures found in fishes.

Here is another, darker, one.

THE RUBY RING

There was a Jew, Shmuel, who was beloved of his king. He always thought carefully before delivering his opinion, which invariably turned out to be right. This drew the ire and then, increasingly, the hatred of the chief counsellor. He schemed to find a way to bring down this upstart Jew. His chance came when the king rewarded Shmuel with a gold ring holding a large fiery ruby for his services to the Crown.

The counsellor arranged for the ring to be stolen. That night, when it was in his hands, he looked with greedy eyes on the fire flickering in the stone. He wanted to keep it for himself but knew that a chance search of his quarters would turn it up. He thought he would put the jewel in a place no one would suspect or discover. He gave orders for it to be taken in a sealed bag aboard a fast sailing ship and thrown overboard at the deepest point off the coast. His spies ensured all went to plan.

Not long after, the counsellor went to the king. 'How do you know that the Jew regards you and your gifts with the same honour you bestow on him? How do you know he hasn't sold off the ruby ring already?' He pushed and pushed the king, until the king could bear it no longer. He sent for Shmuel.

'Shmuel, I find I have need, temporarily, of the ring I gave you. Return it to me in three days. If not ...' he left the rest unsaid. There was no need to say more. The penalty for disobedience of the king's orders was beheading.

Shmuel's knees shook. He was already aware the ring had been stolen. What could he do? He went home to his wife, who consoled him, *gam zeh letova* (this also is for the good). The couple searched their house and grounds again. They sent messengers to all the goldsmiths in the city to see if the ring had been offered for sale. One day went past. There was no news.

The second day drew to a close with no news. Shmuel spent a long time at his prayers, his hands shaking as they wound and rewound the straps of his *tefillin* during the morning prayers.

On the third day Shmuel's wife could bear the tension no longer. She decided as it was Friday, she would go to the fish market as usual and buy a good fish for their last meal together. She spent time over the freshly landed catch, looking for clear eyes and glistening scales. She chose a large firm fish and brought it home to be gutted.

In her kitchen she sliced the fish from tail to head and pulled out a peculiar object, something that no respectable fish should have lodged in its insides. It was a leather bag, heavy with lead seals. She slit it open and screamed for Shmuel to come. He rushed in, dreading to see blood pouring from his wife.

Instead he saw red, the fiery red of the ruby ring. Carefully they washed the ring and polished it until the stone gleamed. 'Thank God,' Shmuel cried, 'thank God.' He kissed his wife and strode off to the palace with the ring tucked in his pocket.

His wife wiped her eyes and calmly continued preparing the fish for Shabbos.

Gam zeh letova. This also is for the good.

When Tobias and Aaron Rozinsky arrived on the shores of Britain in the 1870s they changed their surname to Shepherd after their father's first name, Shepsel. They were escaping being drafted into the Russian army for thirty years each. Instead, they tried to make a living teaching *cheder* in London. When that didn't pan out, they walked west, selling chamois leathers and sponges for horse leathers. Aaron went to Plymouth, Tobias travelled into Wales, stopping at Ystalyfera in the Swansea Valleys. When Aaron was widowed, he joined his brother in Swansea and together they founded Welsh Glass. In 1913 they called their nephew, Jacob Minkes, over to work as a glass beveller. The family moved to Cardiff. Both Leonard Minkes and Ruth, daughter of Harry Clompus, were born and brought up in Cardiff and got married at Cathedral Road Synagogue, Cardiff, on 13 April 1948. Only the frontage remains of what was a beautiful *shul*.

This is Ruth Clompus' story, given to me by her son, John Minkes.

RINGO

Any couple getting engaged, as we did, at Didcot Railway Station, on a cold and clammy October day should perhaps expect the course of true love to run a little awry. And so it did.

On our return to Cardiff, we announced the glad tidings of our engagement to our respective families. Mine were delighted – they had begun to fear that I would never marry! Leonard's parents took the news well, but were quick to point out his new responsibilities. 'You must buy her a ring immediately,' they announced.

I didn't particularly want a ring, but it was too soon to start arguing with my future parents-in-law. So we dutifully went shopping, preferably for an emerald or an antique ring. But emeralds were inordinately expensive and, Victorian fingers being more delicate than mine, no antique ring would fit. In one shop, however, I found something more beautiful than any ring. It was a Dresden plate, in delicate basket-weave, gay with tiny sprigs of flowers. I pleaded, successfully, to be given a large plate in place of a small ring, and radiantly bore my treasure home.

Soon after, a very crestfallen Leonard appeared. His father had greeted him with, 'Well, what kind of a ring did you buy?' On hearing no such transaction had taken place, he was furious.

'Well, I did buy her something instead,' said Leonard defensively.

'Good. What was it?'

'A plate.'

'A PLATE?'

'Yes, but — '

'BUT WHAT?'

'Well, it wasn't a new plate; actually it's an old plate.'

At this, my prospective father-in-law almost had a stroke, and Leonard was impelled to promise that he would buy a ring and make an honest woman of me before leaving Cardiff, next day. After a frantic trek around the few remaining jewellers' shops, we found one ring that fitted; no emeralds, alas! – to save my father-in-law's peace of mind, I settled for diamonds.

I was glad of it during the next few months, while Leonard was working in Geneva. He wrote to me quite often, but in true academic fashion, forgot to post most of the letters. If not for that twinkling ring, I should have assumed that he had changed his mind, but didn't know how to end the affair. However, as an economist, having made his enormous investment, his conscience would surely force him to follow through!

And so it proved. He returned in time for the wedding, reasonably sound in mind, limb and heart. Choosing a wedding ring proved surprisingly simple: we bought one from the man who had sold us the Dresden plate. Even the wedding day went comparatively smoothly, until suddenly, in the midst of the celebrations, Leonard said, 'Where is your wedding ring?' I looked at my left hand – no ring! Pandemonium broke out: women offered me their rings – too small, every one! The hall was searched and interesting items discovered, but not, alas, my ring.

Once again, my father-in-law went purple. It wasn't enough to have a son and daughter-in-law who bought plates instead of rings; now they would begin married life by giving everyone the impression that they were living in sin! We promised to buy a ring as soon as the shops opened, but his face was still clouded as we drove away. Fortunately, we found a replacement for the missing badge of respectability before flying to Geneva, so I could meet my new friends and neighbours correctly dressed!

Some weeks later, we arranged to meet some friends who were visiting Switzerland. To my surprise, they handed me a little package. There, wrapped in tissue paper, lay my first wedding ring. Another friend who had been taking photographs had helped me out of the car and my ring had fallen off into his camera case and lain there undiscovered, until he removed the film for developing. But what to do with it? Fortunately, it was a plain ring and in Switzerland many men wore rings. So now you know why my husband wears a wedding ring – it's because we are a wee bit absent-minded!

๑✛๑

The Jews have lived in Cardiff since 1787. They worked as watchmakers, carpenters, jewellers and shopkeepers. As the community grew and prospered, they built synagogues, Orthodox and Reform, moving with the population from Bute to Grangetown to Penylan and Cyncoed. The Marquis of Bute donated land for the first Jewish burials. As we age we tend to fall back on our memories, our childhood. We are falling into a time where superstition is becoming prevalent again, perhaps in direct relation to the uncertainties that face us.

Del Reid has gifted me this personal story.

The Red Ribbon

Del had been invited down to Penylan House in Cardiff, a Jewish nursing home, to give a talk on superstition in Judaism. His wife and young daughter came with him to participate in another activity earlier on in the day.

The home used the dining hall as its activity room and bingo was played there on Tuesday nights. It had a wide glass doorway out to the vestibule and the stairs leading to the bedrooms, and two swing doors opposite to allow free access to the kitchen when serving and clearing away.

Del was set up on the free wall between the two sides on a low stage. His wife and daughter settled down on the side with some toys.

He had just begun his talk about the old ways and had several elders nodding with recognition that their parents or grandparents had done similar. An old lady got out of her chair, crossed in front of him and went into the kitchen. She emerged the other side and cricked up the stairs. Not long after she came down, reversed the process and walked across in front of Del to present his daughter with a teddy bear. She then sat down with a sigh of satisfaction.

Del was bemused but carried on. Not long after, another old lady, sat behind the first, got up, crossed in front of Del, took the bear off his daughter, walked back across, through the kitchen door, out the other side and *krikhed* up the stairs.

She returned, went through the one door, out the other, walked in front of Del and presented his daughter with the bear, which now sported a red ribbon. She then walked back to her seat and sat down to listen to the rest of Del's speech.

Afterwards, during the tea and cake, Del asked the care manager what had happened. The red ribbon he understood, it was to ward off evil spirits. New mothers tied a red ribbon around their baby's cot or wrist to remind Lilith of her promise not to eat them. Grandmothers tied a red string round the wrist of their grandchildren going off on long journeys. Sellers held out red strings blessed at the tomb of Rachel, knotted seven times, to ward off evil and protect the young. Those had to be worn until they dropped off.

But why did the second woman think it necessary to tie a red ribbon round the bear there and then? She could have given the ribbon later, during the tea, if she wanted to.

'Ah,' said the care manager, 'those ladies share a room. The second one believes the first is a *yeterhora*.'

Del was astonished. He had never heard someone describing another living person as an evil spirit, literally one who has their evil inclination to the fore. And these women shared the same room!

NEWPORT

Newport's first purpose-built synagogue opened in Francis Street in 1871. Newport served as the focal point for the Jewish communities in the Usk and Ebbw Valleys and Breconshire. The later synagogue in Queen's Hill Crescent housed the flowering of the community between the wars. In the 1960s there were forty Jewish families in Newport, including a minister. The woodland park on Risca Road, Dews Wood, was known locally as Jews Wood as the Jewish burial grounds are at the beginning of the land with an *ohel* on the main road. When the synagogue closed in 1999, the *ohel* was used for services until 2006. The *ohel* has a plaque dedicated to Philip (Feivel) Caller,* president of the congregation and of the *Chevra Kadisha* through whose efforts the building was erected in 1954. Now the cemetery can be visited on application.

This tale is a mixture of truth and a Sephardi tale of Eliyahu HaNavi (Elijah the Prophet) who is said to visit those in need, in a variety of disguises, testing their morals and often bestowing magical gifts. He is recognised by his rosy cheeks.

OLD BOOTS

My grandfather, Feivel, came to South Wales with his older brother in 1911. He was 13. They had walked a long, long way. They had walked from their *shtetl* in the district of Grodno, Lithuania, then part of the Russian Empire. They had walked until they hit the

---

* Pronounced Ka-ler.

sea and took passage on a boat. They hoped to get to America, the *goldene medina*. They landed in England. There the immigration officers, fed up of the foreign names they battled to understand, gave them names more pleasing to the English ear. My grandfather Feivel became Philip. His brother Wolf became Barney. After a welcome cup of tea and a sandwich from the Jewish Welfare Board in London they started walking and didn't stop until they came to South Wales. In Cardiff they found a room to share. Uncle Barney left Feivel to go and buy up some odds and sods, trinkets and haberdashery. He put them all in a backpack and gave them to my grandfather to sell.

'Go up the valleys. There's lots of housewives who can't get down to Cardiff. They'll be glad to buy the stuff.'

So Feivel shouldered the pack, took a bottle of tea with him and the hard heel of the bread and caught a bus up the Rhondda Valley. All day he walked from door to door selling his wares. Not until nightfall did he catch the bus back down to Cardiff to the room they shared. He gave the money to his brother, who went out early the next morning and bought more stuff to put in the pack.

All day Feivel walked up the rows of houses that lined the hillsides. All day he walked down the rows of houses that followed the colliery trail. He sold to old women, young women, bored women, happy women. He chatted in Yiddish, he chatted in English, he chatted in Welsh. And in none of these languages was he understood, his accent was so strong, but they laughed and they bought. Not a lot, but enough to give him money for the bus back down to Splott in Cardiff, where they had a room and enough to buy more for the morning.

One day he walked up the valley from Pontypridd, where there were some Jews. He walked up to Treharris through Troed-y-rhiw until he reached Merthyr Tydfil. He knew in Merthyr he'd be able to get another bite to eat from one of the Jewish houses. He walked back as the wind blew, the rain fell and the sheep wandered over the road. He stopped and sat down for a rest on the banks of the Taff. His feet were hurting. He took one boot off. This boot that had come with him from Lithuania, as had the other. His feet,

though small, had grown as he had. He had reached his adult height that lack of nutrition had granted him … the hugeness that was 5ft 2in, or 157cm in new money. His clothes were clean, as clean as he could get them despite the coal dust blowing across the hillside. He had no food spilled down the front, mainly because he had no food.

He poked a finger through the widening hole in the sole of his boot. He had already lined it with newspaper and the wodge had disintegrated into fluffy bits that fell out behind him like those breadcrumbs Hansel and Gretel left. I'm sure he would have liked the breadcrumbs to eat rather than leave them for the birds. He dangled his foot in the cool water. Such a pleasure.

Well, if one was feeling the benefit so should the other. He took off his other boot. This one flapped like a bird with a broken wing. The sole and the upper were no longer related. Feivel sighed. He still had the next valley to walk before he could crawl to the bus and get down to Cardiff and Barney, who waited for him.

He pulled out of his pack his bottle of tea and hard heel of bread. For a moment he contemplated soaking the bread in the tea to save his teeth. Then he shook his head.

'If you don't fancy it, I'll have it,' said a voice at his elbow in Yiddish.

Feivel turned his head, astonished that someone had crept up on him. He saw a small thin man with rosy cheeks and a long white beard. Feivel could see white sidelocks curled around his ears under the soft felt hat crammed on his head. The man looked as if he hadn't eaten for weeks. Feivel thought the rosiness might be due to TB. This man needs the bread more than I do, he thought.

'Please,' said Feivel, holding out the bread, 'I haven't said the blessing yet.'

'Thank you, you're a *mentsch*,' said the stranger, taking the bread and whispering a quick blessing before sucking on the hard crust. Feivel offered him the bottle of tea to wash the bread down. The old man nodded his thanks and slurped eagerly.

Feivel turned his gaze back to the sluggish Taff, soaking his poor feet.

All the while the old man chattered of this and that and Feivel answered as best he could. The old man handed him the bottle of tea back. Feivel wiped the mouth and then drank.

'If I could reward you, what would you want? Gold? The love of the most beautiful woman? Deep learning in the Torah?'

Feivel laughed. 'What would I do with my life if I had gold? There would be nothing to strive for. Every woman I meet is the most beautiful when I meet her, it's only after a while she pales. And what would I do with such learning? There are no courts of rabbis here in this country.' He waved his arms wildly at the steep hillside and ravaged valleys around him.

'Then what do you desire most in the world?' asked the old man. 'I'm curious, a young man like you who doesn't want these things.'

'What I want is a pair of stout boots that fit. That would make my life complete.'

'You're in luck,' said the old man. 'As it happens, I have in my pack a pair of the stoutest boots that I think might be just your size.' He drew out the boots and put them on the grass. 'Try them on.'

Feivel shook his head. 'I can't, my feet …'

'Are nice and clean from the water. Dry them on your shirt and try them on.'

Urged on by the old man, Feivel tried one boot and then the other. Whether it was because his feet were cooled by the water and not so swollen despite the newness of the boots, they felt as soft as lambswool. He stood up and walked a few steps away from the bank.

'They're a perfect fit! I won't be happy in my old boots now. You've spoiled me forever.' Feivel turned to the old man.

The man wasn't there. Feivel looked up the road and down. There was nowhere to hide. He could see down the valley and up the hillside. No one. Not even a sheep.

He looked for his old boots. They were gone too. What should he do? Take these new boots off and leave them for someone else, walk back to Cardiff in bare feet, or keep them on? What would you do?

Feivel kept the boots on. His feet felt cushioned, protected. Now his feet didn't hurt, his face didn't wince so much. His patter to the housewives flowed better, his accent less impenetrable. Soon he was selling more. Barney bought a warehouse on the proceeds. Feivel was promoted to a bicycle and eventually a little shop in Tonypandy.

The first day he stood behind the counter in his shop in his brown overalls and his newly shined boots was a happy day. It wasn't long before he married Feigie, who helped him in the shop.

Now Feigie liked the better things in life and she thought that Feivel could give it to her. She liked to be smart, she liked Feivel to be smart, too. She didn't like his boots.

'Feh! As long as I've known you, you've worn the same *farshtunkene* boots. Can't you smarten yourself up a *bisl*?'

Feivel would nod his head and keep wearing the boots. Until he heard not one, not two, but four customers all remark on the fact he was wearing the same boots to *shul*, to weddings, to *bar mitzvahs*, whether they matched his suits or not. By this time, he had a baby son, my father. The young family eventually moved to Preston Road in Newport, where another son was born. Feivel worked hard buying and selling all sorts all over the Rhondda and Rhymney Valleys.

He bought a pair of shoes for best. They were of soft Italian leather. Somehow, though, they didn't feel as comfortable as his old boots that were worn in all the right places. But seeing them on his feet made Feigie happy.

'Good,' she exclaimed. 'Now you can throw away the old boots. Get yourself a new pair of working shoes. You don't need to show how hard you worked to get where you are.' She picked up the boots, worn in all the right places and put them down by the back door. 'You can take them to the Turkish baths and leave them for someone who needs them,' she ordered.

The next time Feivel went to the Turkish baths, he left the boots behind after his soak. That night there was a knocking on the door when they sat down to eat. Feivel opened the door to a young lad.

'Here, Mr Caller, these belong to you. You left them behind in the baths. Everyone knows they're yours.' He held out the pair of boots. Feivel took them and gave the boy a penny for his trouble.

The boots were left on newspaper on the black and white tiles in the kitchen. After their soak in the steam room, the leather on the boots had dried out and was beginning to crack a little. Feigie curled her nose as the leather curled.

'Get them out of my kitchen!' she cried.

Feivel loved fishing. He often supplemented their diet by the fish he caught. So no one was surprised when one day he set off with his equipment: his rod, reel, lures, bait and basket. When he had finished for the day, Feivel looked around to check no one was watching up and down the bank. Then he pulled the boots out of his basket and threw them one at a time into the Usk. The water was flowing fast at this point and he thought no one would find them. He went home to Feigie happy.

They had just sat down to their evening meal when there was a knock at the back door. Standing outside, refusing to come in because of the state of their boots, which were very muddy, were two old fishermen. Feivel knew them from the angling club he had recently joined. They were very pleased. They handed Feivel a wet bag. 'Here, these belongs to you. We recognised them straightaway. Couldn't think how they ended up in the river.'

Feivel stretched out a hand and gingerly took the bag containing his boots. He thanked the men and gave them the price of a couple of pints for their trouble.

Feigie refused to have them in the house. They languished in the outhouse, slimy and stinking from the river. Feivel was under orders to do something about them and quickly. He scratched his head. He had tried everything. He looked around for an idea. Then it came to him.

That night he crept out of the house with only a lantern to guide him. He picked up a bag and a spade from the outhouse and stumbled his way down the narrow back garden. Near the back wall under an apple tree he dug a hole and buried the bag inside. Patting the earth down, he picked up the lantern and returned to the house.

What he didn't know that his neighbour had watched the whole proceedings from an upstairs window, behind a net curtain. If Neighbourhood Watch had been invented then, this neighbour would have been first on the list. She was already suspicious of the foreigners who had moved in next door. Now she was certain Feivel had murdered someone and buried them in the garden.

The following morning, just as Feivel was going off to work, a knock came at the front door. Two policemen stood there.

'We've had a complaint that you've buried a body in your garden, Mr Caller. All right if we come in and have a look?'

Feivel hung his head. He couldn't have looked more guilty if he tried.

'Follow me, officers,' he said. 'I'll just get the spade.'

He walked down the garden with the bemused police trailing behind. At the bottom the newly turned earth told its own story. One of the policemen took the spade and began to dig. When the hessian bag surfaced with its wet and stained patches, both police looked at each other. Carefully now the rest of the bag was unearthed and opened.

'You see, gentlemen, my wife won't have them in the house,' explained Feivel. 'I've tried getting rid of them but they keep coming back. What else was I supposed to do?'

After cups of tea and slices of Feigie's Victoria sponge, the policemen left, telling Feivel not to bury his boots again. Feigie was so relieved that he wasn't being arrested that she dried the boots and wrapped them up in an old pillowcase. She put them in the bottom of Feivel's wardrobe.

And that's where they stayed until he died. Knowing the story, one boot went to one son, and one to the other. My father had four children. When he died, the boot was divided up between us. My older brother had the sole, my sister the upper, my younger brother the heel and I had the tongue, which I've used to tell you this tale.

Schnorrers are Jewish beggars. They have been with us forever. There is a long tradition in Judaism of caring for the poor, but then there is the poor and the professional poor. Professional beggars, *schnorrers*, have long gone down in legend for their cunning in getting money, food and what they want out of the people. Nowadays they knock on your door just before the festivals asking for money for others. You can count on them year on year. They have favourite runs. One lone *schnorrer* who lived in the local asylum in Newport used to turn up at a back door on the odd occasion and after he had his handout would ask for the daughter's hand in marriage. Needless to say, she never consented.

This is one of many stories about Hershel Ostropolier, a giant bear of a man. He was taken into the court of the grandson of the Baal Shem Tov of Medzhybizh, the founder of Hassidism, to entertain him as Rabbi Boruch was prone to depression. Stories of Hershel's wit, pranks and jokes have become legend. He was often depicted as a *schnorrer*, who would turn up asking for alms right about the time the dinner was being put on the table. Many a housewife shut her shutters and hid until she thought Hershel had passed by, only to find him lurking under her windows sniffing the air.

'Lovely gefilte fish you've fried today. Couldn't help wondering if you had one spare, for a poor man?'

He walked around the town, knocking on doors, or wandered from stall to stall in the market square. No feast was complete until he turned up, hand outstretched for his penny.

LIKE FATHER, LIKE SON

One day Hershel had walked a long way on the road from one town to another. He stopped for the night at an inn. He didn't have any money to pay for the room so he was given a place in the stable. The innkeeper refused to give him any food. The stable was enough.

'That's alright,' said Hershel, 'I'll just have to do what my father did when this kind of thing happened to him.'

'Really?' asked the innkeeper's wife.

'Yes,' said Hershel, smiling sadly, 'I'll just have to do what my father did.'

And he went to the stables and lay down, pulling a horse blanket over his body.

The innkeeper and his wife locked up and went to bed. The wife tossed and turned. She nudged her husband.

'Are you awake?'

'I am now,' he said.

'What did he mean … he'd do what his father did? He's out there in our barn. He could set it on fire if he's cross. What if his father had a bad temper? He's a bear of a man. What if he inherited his father's temper and broke up the stables and then …'

Her husband tried to get back to sleep but his wife kept waking him up with more fanciful ideas.

'He could murder us in our beds if we upset him. We didn't feed him. Perhaps if we fed him, he'd leave us alone. What do you think?'

'I think that if you're so worried, feed him and then I can get to sleep,' answered her husband, who then rolled over.

The woman got up and made a plate of meat and potatoes. She took it out to the stables and woke Hershel. He scoffed the plate of food down and washed it through with ale. He thanked the woman, who smiled and went back to her bed, eased in her mind.

In the morning, after a hearty breakfast, Hershel was ready to set off. He had just taken a few steps away from the inn when the innkeeper's wife came running out after him.

'Tell me, please, what did your father do?'

'Ah,' laughed Hershel, 'why, he went to bed hungry. What else do you think he did?' He whistled as he walked off down the road, patting his full belly.

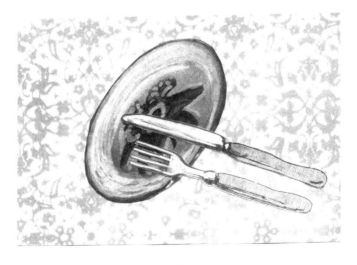

Dawlish

During the Second World War children in Britain were evacuated from the big cities to the small towns and villages in the country-side. Jewish children were no exception. A group of around forty Jewish children were evacuated to a Jewish hostel at 3 East Cliff Road, Dawlish in Devon, in 1941. The hostel was run by Levi Gertiner and his wife, who had come from Palestine. They ran the hostel on kibbutz lines with communal duties for all who lived there as well as lessons including Hebrew. The children attended the local schools and gathered together every Shabbat, when in the late afternoon they were told stories. Shirley Selsdon was 10 when she arrived and stayed there for four years. This story made a strong impression on her.

The Three Who Ate on Yom Kippur

In a little *shtetl* not far from Cracow the Jewish community had suffered a huge blow. Cholera had run rife through the houses, bringing death in its wake.

Most of the people had lost someone and they were now all in a weak state. As Rosh Hashonnah came and went the devout people struggled to find apples and honey to welcome in the new year with sweetness. They cried as Yom Kippur arrived nine days later and the fast began. Some found it difficult to sit on the wooden benches in the synagogue. Some, when they fell to their knees on this holiest day, were too weak to stand again and had to be helped up by fellow congregants. And yet they continued to fast, to afflict their bodies as well as their souls.

The rabbi looked around his congregation. He named so many former members during *Yiskor*, the prayer for the souls of the dead, in the late morning. He shook his head and wept. What could he do? He dreaded his congregants dying while in prayer on this most holy day but it seemed so likely.

He thought hard and prayed for guidance. Then he called his *shammes* and warden and sent them off with instructions. He continued the service, tears running down his cheeks, his prayers more fervent as the responses from the others grew less each time.

Eventually the *shammes* and warden returned, carrying three plates of steaming food. The rabbi sat down and invited the *shammes* and warden to sit with him. Then he started to eat and encouraged the other two to eat, too. His congregation looked on in horror. A rabbi eating on Yom Kippur! Unheard of!

The rabbi ate steadily. 'It is a Jew's duty to choose life,' he said. 'Eat and live!'

His congregants each accepted a morsel of food and then the rabbi sent them home to eat with their families and get well. The three continued to eat and wept as they did so. *L'chayim*; to life!

PLYMOUTH

In the logs of Sir Francis Drake is mention of his quartermaster and navigator from the Barbican, Plymouth: the Jew, Moses the Navigator. Moses sailed with Drake all around the world.

Plymouth became a stopping place for Jewish seamen, merchants and traders. Eventually, a small community was established. By 1762 the synagogue was built in Catherine Street, facing away from the road. The Holy Ark was flat-packed and delivered from the Netherlands before being built in situ. The *bimah*, the platform for reading the Torah scrolls, was built by carpenters from the dockyard and resembles naval construction on ships at the time. The *shul* is now the oldest Ashkenazi synagogue still in constant use in the English-speaking world. Exeter synagogue, 40 miles up the road, was built the following year.

The small naval town of Devonport, connected to Plymouth, also had a synagogue. The Jews in Devonport considered themselves not more important but so devout that they couldn't walk the several miles from one place to the other on the Sabbath. One family, the Fredmans, were typical of the immigrant families around Britain. The parents came in, as poor as can be, working all the hours they could so their children could have an education and improve their lot in life. Myer Fredman, one of their sons, became Mayor of Devonport. He was so observant, in order to get to synagogue on a Shabbat morning, he would leave his coin to pass the tollgate on Halfpenny Bridge the evening before.

Plymouth was also a place of succour, as this tale shows.

The Smell of Kugel

In September 1891 the Dutch passenger steamship *Dubbeldam*, on its way to New York, limped into Plymouth harbour suffering from severe problems. Bad weather had caused its passengers to be battened down for several days. Among the passengers were 180 destitute Russian Jews fleeing the clearances of the Pale of Settlement. They were in a parlous state. The Jewish community of Plymouth rushed into action organising collections of clothing from the people of Plymouth at large, who gave freely. They also asked the captain if they could provide kosher food for the passengers. Captain Potjer not only allowed this but insisted that the ship's company could and would pay for it.

Mrs Spiers and Mrs Levy went into overdrive and spent two days and nights cooking the 150lb of meat for the half-starved passengers. Myer Fredman, Asher Levy and others delivered the soup, meat, bread and other comestibles to the people on board.

As they saw the passengers sit down to the first kosher meal they had had in a long time, the Plymothians were visibly moved. Especially when one old man held up his tin of soup and sniffed long and hard.

'*Oy, mechaye nefashos*. This is wonderful. We have been living off herring and little else for more than a month. Just the smell alone is enough to revive me. Perhaps to thank you, I can tell you a little story, yes?'

The Plymothians settled down, for Jews everywhere love a story. The old man slurped his soup, then waved his bony arm.

'Once there was a wealthy merchant who had everything to make life sweet, a prosperous business, a good house and a wife he loved very much. You'd think he'd be satisfied, no? No. He lacked a child, more specifically a son to say *kaddish* over him when he died. The merchant had been married for ten years and no sign of a child, let alone a son. He was in despair. He decided to go to the local Hassidic rabbi and ask him to grant a *get*, a divorce.

'Early the next morning he rushed to the rabbi's house. The rabbi was still at his prayers and his wife asked the merchant to take a seat in the anteroom. The merchant sat down to wait. Soon he could smell something delicious. He recognised the aroma of a potato *kugel*. How he loved *kugel*. He drew in a deep breath to capture the smell of the grated potato and onion mixture cooking in the *rebbetzin*'s kitchen.

'As he waited for the rabbi he enjoyed the smell of the *kugel*. The rabbi passed the door but didn't come in. Hours passed and still the merchant sat there, the tantalising aroma tickling his nostrils.

'By the afternoon the merchant was feeling decidedly hungry. Eventually the rabbi arrived and beckoned him into his study. There, on the table, was a plate with a slice of steaming *kugel* and a fork. The rabbi indicated the plate was for the merchant, who didn't wait for a second invitation. He guzzled the piece of *kugel* down as fast as possible. Me, I'd get a stomach ache. Him, the rabbi looked him in the eye and granted him his *get*! None of the merchant's practised speech was necessary.

'Not long after the merchant married again. This wife produced children, six of them in quick succession. Was he happy? Six children, such a blessing! But no, these children were all … girls! Not a boy among them. No one to say *kaddish* for him.

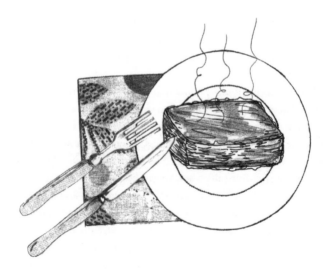

'Off the merchant went, back to the rabbi's house. Again, the *rebbetzin* was baking *kugel*. The succulent aroma filled the house. The merchant sniffed and drew a deep breath in. The smell was so wonderful. He couldn't wait to get inside the rabbi's study and be offered another piece of *kugel*.

'The merchant slowly savoured his mouthful of steaming *kugel*. The only time the rabbi spoke was to grant the merchant his second *get*. Without a word from him! The merchant went home happy.

'He married for a third time. And what do you know? You know it, his wife gave birth to a boy. Oy, was that boy cossetted and spoiled. He was the apple of his father's eye, his crown, his *kaddish*. His father doted on him. At the age of 5, the boy asked his father if he could come on the next trip. And the merchant could deny him nothing.

'Father and son set sail. The wind was fair until they were far away from land. A storm arose, like the one that Jonah went down with, like the one we encountered on our way here. No matter how he tried, the merchant couldn't keep his son safe. The ship broke up and many lives were lost.

'In agony the merchant returned to the rabbi's house and howled out his pain. Why did he go through all the *gittin*, the heartache, only to lose his greatest treasure? The rabbi asked him to taste the *kugel* on the plate in front of him.

'"How can I eat at a time like this? Rabbi, if I'd known … all those years ago when I came to you …"'

'"What do you mean, years ago?" asked the rabbi. "You came this morning and fell asleep waiting for me. Here, eat the *kugel*."

'The merchant couldn't believe his ears. He asked the date and was astounded to find it was the day he had come to ask for his first *get*. He didn't understand what had happened.

'"The smell of the *kugel* transported you to a possible future. You saw many years in the time it took for the *kugel* to bake. Go home and kiss your wife. Be happy." The rabbi smiled and patted the merchant on the back.

'The merchant went home, sobered and sad. He resigned himself to never having children. But you know and I know what happened, eh? You're right. Eventually his wife, his first and only wife, gave birth to a child … a son!'

The old man stopped. He returned to his meal with gusto. The Plymothian Jews were humbled by his story.

The following week, when the steamer was repaired and ready to continue on to New York, Myer Fredman, Asher Levy and members of the committee returned. They presented the captain with a silver fuse-box inscribed:

> Capt. Andries Potjer, for sympathetic treatment of emigrant Russian Jews under his care, Plymouth, 1891.

As the *Jewish Chronicle* reported at the time:

> Mr. Asher Levy, in making the presentation, thanked Captain Potjer for the kind manner in which he had assisted the committee in their endeavours to alleviate the condition of their distressed brethren. These thanks were not to be considered as only emanating from the small community at Plymouth, but came from the Jews of the world, who noted and appreciated such acts of kindness. Captain Potjer's skill in navigating his damaged vessel safely into a port of refuge was only excelled by the consideration he had exhibited for every class of passenger on board. The intrinsic value of the gift was small, but he trusted Captain Potjer would carry it round the world with him, and keep it as a memento of incidents in connection with his visit to Plymouth.

The internal story has been attributed to wonder-working rabbis but mostly Menachem Mendel, Rav of Lubavitch, grandson of the founder of Chabad, Shneur Zalman.

PENZANCE

There had long been a Jewish presence in Penzance due to its exports of tin, copper and the like attracting merchants. Some say that Market Jew Street is named for the Jews who lived there. Rabbi Bernard Susser* suggested Marazion was an ancient Jewish trading centre, named for 'sight of Zion' or 'bitterness of Zion'. Marazion was 'anciently known' as Market-Jew. And Market Jew Street, Penzance, was the road leading to Marazion.

Jews, so they say, had been brought to Cornwall as slaves after the Bar Kochba revolt of 135CE and put to work in the mines. A single Domitian coin found in a mining gallery is the source for this. Perhaps this explains the number of Cornish tales of unseen Jewish miners, who have to keep working except on Saturdays, Easter Monday and Christmas Eve and are working there still, known as the knockers.

Most later Jews were traders or clockmakers. Lemon Hart, who was born in Penzance, made his name and fortune supplying rum to the British Navy, supposedly the reason why the Navy ordered each sailor to have a tot daily. And the Lemon Hart clock in Penzance was supplied by him, too. The first synagogue was built in 1768.

This family story is from Anthony Joseph.

---

* *The Jews of South-West England*, Rabbi Bernard Susser.

FINGERING VICTORY

'Tell me how you lost your finger fighting alongside Nelson at Trafalgar again, *Zaide*!'

Rabbi Barnett Asher Simmons lifted up his little grandson and sat him on his knee.

'Well, it was like this. I had been press-ganged into the Royal Navy from the streets of Penzance. Chapel Street to be precise. I was 19 years old and an apprentice sign painter.'

'Is that why you were put on Admiral Nelson's ship?'

'The *Victory*, yes, I think it might be, a couple of years later. But there was no time for painting in the roar of battle. Cannon, gunshots, smoke, fire all surrounding us in noise and fear. The battle raged for five hours. French were falling and our men, too. Shooting, shouting, so much noise and confusion. In the midst of all this I felt a sharp pain and looked down at my hand. You don't want to hear the gruesome details.' He looked at his grandson with a twinkle in his eye.

'I do, I do,' insisted the boy. 'Tell me again how you wrapped a greasy rag from a torn sail round your hand to stop the blood. And when all was quiet, when Lord Nelson was dying, you realised you'd lost a finger.'

'Ah, well, if you know so much, you don't need me to tell you, do you?'

'Stop filling the boy's head with nonsense, Dad.' His daughter had come in the room to fetch her wayward son. 'I believed that tale of yours, too, until Mama told me you'd lost it in a boating accident in Penzance Harbour.' She shooed her son. 'Go find your grandmother in the kitchen. She might have some milk for you and maybe something else.' The boy ran off happy.

'Who knows which is true? Only the Almighty. I wasn't married to your mother until 1813.'

'In Penzance, wasn't it? If you were the rabbi of Penzance, who married you?'

'I wasn't the rabbi then. I kept being employed and then unemployed by the congregation. First, they wanted a rabbi, then they

wanted a *shochet* and a *mohel*, then all, then none. And then we start the whole thing again. And all the time I have to make a living too, selling crockery and bones.

'Bluma was from Redruth, but in the end Rabbi Lipman from Falmouth married us in Penzance. We spent so many years there. You were born there, so were your brothers and sisters, all eleven of you.

'And it was a long streak of *tzores*. Always complaining the congregation was, nothing good enough for them. Not as a rabbi, not as a slaughterer, you should have heard them talk about butchering the meat! There were no complaints about my circumcising the baby boys, thank God, but they did mutter about the records I kept. No wonder I became ill.

'And then when they were done with me, they asked me back because no none else would come and take my place. Forty years I worked for them. Forty years, enough already. And now we are here, with you in Merthyr Tydfil. And here we shall stay.'

'Um, well, saying that … a message has come from Penzance. They want you back.'

FALMOUTH

Here is another family story from Anthony Joseph. Barnet was a common Anglicised name among Ashkenazi Jews. Many inns in the South West accommodated Jewish pedlars who stayed overnight by keeping a locked cupboard with kosher utensils inside, so the traveller could make a meal for himself.

THE AMIDAH HORSE

Barnet Levy couldn't find work as a soap boiler in London. The Guilds were too strong. He had not long arrived from Alsace-Lorraine and was desperate to earn money. Someone told him that there was a Jew down in Falmouth who set pedlars up, financing a box of trinkets and small goods and, wonder of wonders, even a horse to carry the heavy box. Barnet didn't wait. He got himself down to Falmouth as fast as he could. He carried dry bread in his pocket and a bottle for his drink. He was half starved when he arrived at the silversmith's door more than a week later.

'*Bistu* Zender Falmouth?'

'I am Alexander Moses, yes,' came the answer. Barnet had found him. He almost collapsed with relief. 'Come in, don't leave him standing on the doorstep,' Alexander's wife, Phoebe (Feygele), encouraged him to come in and sit to eat. Barnet's hand touched the *mezuzah* on the right-hand lintel of the door briefly before kissing his fingertips as he entered.

He rushed to wash in the scullery, pouring the water over his hands and saying the blessing. He sat at the table and waited until Alexander had said the blessing over the bread, *hamotzi*.

'Well, young man, what are you here for?' asked Alexander, handing him a piece of bread with salt on.

Barnet chewed slowly as he thought what to say. He knew that for this man, only the truth would do. 'I've come to find work. I'll do anything. But I won't break Shabbes.'

'Feh! Who asked you? You think because we live so far away from a big city, we can't keep Shabbes or kosher? Did you ask what kind of meat you're eating?' Alexander was disdainful.

Barnet scrambled backwards in his haste to reassure his host. 'No, no, I'd heard, I knew … you have a *mezuzah* …' he trailed off miserably.

Phoebe came to his rescue. 'He's teasing you. We are kosher and we keep Shabbes. We've even started a *shul* here. But tell me, do you have any news of my cousins? Last time I heard from them was nearly three months ago. Sometimes I really miss Alsace, especially when it rains here. It rains here a lot.' She handed him a plate of delicious smelling food.

Over the course of the meal Barnet imparted the news from home and Alexander formed an opinion of the young man. After they had *benched*, he spoke.

'If you are willing to work hard, then I have an opportunity for you. I am a silversmith. I make nice things. I make pretty things. I have a shop to sell them. But I can only reach those people who come into town. There are so many villages and towns with people who would love to buy my goods and other items but they have no means of transport. I will fill you a box with trinkets and other stuff. I will pay for a horse for you. You go off round the countryside, here in Cornwall and even Devon and sell my stuff. I will pay you a wage. Now, what do you say?'

'Where will I live? Where will I spend Shabbes? How will I eat?'

'All good questions. We take them in turn. You will live in a room here in Falmouth, I know a very nice woman who takes in lodgers. She keeps a kosher kitchen for me. Don't abuse her trust. You will spend Shabbes here as often as not, or in one of the inns we have an arrangement with. And that's where you'll eat, too. I'll give you a list.' He stood up. 'Now, I think you need some sleep. Come.'

In the morning Barnet came face to face with the horse of which he would become so fond. He heaved a box up onto its back and buckled it on tightly. He was scared it would fall off before he left Falmouth, climbing the winding lanes up onto the cliff path. In his pocket was a list of recommended inns and a list of villages. He had directions to the first one in his head. Before he had left his lodging he had said his morning prayer. He was ready for this.

After midday he stopped the horse and got off so he could say the afternoon prayers. He took three steps back to finish the *Amidah*, the central standing prayer. He had found the first village and had sold one item. Not much but a start. Then he was off again to the next village and the inn for the night.

Well before dusk, he clopped into the yard of the inn. He presented his letter from Zender Falmouth and was shown a locked cupboard. The innkeeper opened it. Inside were kosher cooking utensils. Barnet pulled out a frying pan. On the bottom in chalk

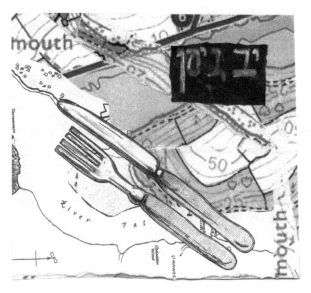

was the name Samuel, the date, and in Hebrew the first lines of the *sedra*, the portion of the Torah, read the week before. The innkeeper allowed him use of the fire and sold him a couple of eggs. Together with cheese and a slice of the bread he had brought with him he made himself a meal. After he had washed up, he wrote his name, the date, and in Hebrew the first lines of this week's *sedra* in chalk on the bottom of the utensils. He put them all back in the cupboard and watched the innkeeper lock the cupboard back up. He fell into his bed after saying his prayers with a smile on his lips. This work he could do.

Wherever he had to stop for the night the same pattern followed. He mentioned Zender Falmouth and the innkeeper led him to a locked cupboard. He wrote his name, date, and Hebrew text in chalk on the bottom of the pans and utensils. He got to know the names of the pedlars who were a week ahead of him. He returned to Falmouth as often as he could in time for Shabbes. He changed his name under Alexander's instruction to a more Anglicised one to fit in. Alexander offered to make a *shidduch*, a match with his niece in London. Barnet thought it was about time. He set off.

His return journey was much easier than his outward. But once he hit London he despaired. Where would he find this girl? The houses were so crowded and rounded back on each other. It was a maze. He went from door to door, asking, asking. Finally, he was directed to a door. He knocked. A young woman opened the door and asked, '*Junge, vos vunches du?*'*Barnet fell in love immediately. She was the one. And indeed she was. Barnet and Esther were married and set off back to Falmouth.

Such a strong-willed woman he'd married, Esther couldn't bear to be closed up in a carriage with others for more than a week; she insisted that she ride behind him on his horse. They travelled like that all the way to Falmouth. Alexander had arranged a larger room for the young couple and they were satisfied. But Esther knew that with a bit of encouragement Barnet could make something of

---

* Young man, what do you want/wish for?

himself. Alexander had promised that he would stake them on a small shop if they could find the wherewithal.

Barnet set off round the villages and towns with a will. He didn't want to waste a minute. Stopping to dismount and then remount for his afternoon prayers took too much time when he could be in a village selling more trinkets or small goods, making money for his Esther. What to do, what to do?

His long-suffering horse was now taught to take three steps backwards when Barnet finished the *Amidah*, while Barnet swayed on his back, still travelling, still praying. It shaved time off and Barnet did make more sales. Until one day the horse stumbled on his backwards steps and the unaware man, in the middle of his prayer, found himself slipping off the horse into a ditch. *Oy vey!* That was the end of that experiment.

TRURO

Cornwall's newest Jewish community, Kehillat Kernow,* is like the villages and towns in Cornwall. There are some stalwarts who live in the county all year round and keep the place going. And then there are the summer visitors and those who have a second home in Cornwall, visiting every now and then during the year, hoping there will be a service in Truro when they're down. A Torah scroll that had been in the safekeeping of Truro museum was returned for repair and use to Kehillat Kernow. It had come from the defunct Falmouth synagogue. The parade led through the streets of Truro by a Cornish piper, the *sefer* Torah carried under a *khuppa*, was something to behold. The Duke of Gloucester was there for the official restitution, whilst the men all wore their Cornish *kippot*, skullcaps with the yellow Cornish tartan. What a *simcha*!

Here is a well-known Hassidic story set appropriately in a Cornish cottage.

The Cramped Cottage

A young couple and their two children decided they wanted to live the life down in Cornwall. They left their London suburb and travelled down to their new home, an old fisherman's cottage, three squashed bedrooms up the steep stairs and two rooms downstairs

---

* Kehillat meaning a Jewish Community, Kernow being Cornish for Cornwall. Members live in villages and towns across Cornwall coming together for services in Truro.

with the bathroom added on to the back. They didn't mind as they were near the sea, they could see it rushing at them every high tide and could spend lots of time walking on the beach or surfing. The children loved it. They went to a local primary school, walking past hedgerows full of spring and summer flowers, brambles and wild garlic. The parents got used to the daily commute up the steep winding lanes with passing places before they even got to a main road. They even kept in touch with their London community, speaking to the rabbi once a month.

The quaintness of the cottage began to become a pain. The village shop was closed in winter, making getting a loaf of bread or a bottle of milk an expedition. Tempers were shortening in direct ratio to the time it took to get out in the mornings. With four people in a small, cramped cottage life was noisy and fractious.

The monthly call to the rabbi was an oasis of calm. 'What can I do, Rabbi?' asked the father.

'You need some support. Ask your parents to come down and give you some help. They'll jump at the chance.'

The couple discussed it and finally the wife gave in and his parents came down to help. They moved into one of the bedrooms and the two children were put together. The queue for the toilet in the morning stretched into the kitchen. The wife bit her tongue really hard as her mother-in-law offered to clean out the under stairs cupboard where they had stuffed everything lying around before the visitors came. The husband's father sat in his favourite chair and read the paper before him. They went out for walks up to the Cheesewring, across Bodmin Moor, along the South West coastal path but the wind blew and the rain came down too frequently to enjoy them, knowing there was a guilt trip after each one.

The call went into the rabbi after two weeks. 'Rabbi, is this really such a good idea? It's driving my wife mad.'

'Good, good,' said the rabbi. 'You live in such a wonderful place and I think to make sure there's no jealousy, invite your parents-in-law to come and stay as well. They'll feel so much more part of the family. No need to cause *broygus* if you can avoid it.'

The husband was unsure and so was his wife when he discussed it with her. But because he had asked the question in the first place they had to abide by what the rabbi said. You see, if you ask a rabbi a question you have to accept his answer. If you don't want that answer you shouldn't have asked the question in the first place.

So her parents came down with suitcases, food and kisses. Not for their *mechutn*. Her parents had the pull-out-sofa bed in the front room. They had to put it away every day or wait until everyone had gone to bed before pulling it out and going to bed themselves. The children weren't the only ones tiptoeing past in the night to get to the bathroom. There was a lot of ice in the air even though the weather was sultry. Smiles were sprinkled on the children but not the adults.

A fight nearly broke out over the dusters and the hob. Saucepans were banged and dishes washed up before the food was eaten. 'Oh, I thought you'd had a bad day, I was doing you a favour.'

'If you don't want my help all you had to do was say.'

'I don't want to get in the way, I know when I'm not wanted, but we were asked to come down, you know.'

Walks were taken separately with one grandchild each. Instructions were called out to the children to be careful as they went surfing near Newquay, contradicting each other.

It was a week before the call went to the rabbi.

'Rabbi, my parents and my parents-in-law hardly speak to each other. We're walking on eggshells waiting for the bomb to drop and it does frequently in hissing fits. I don't think this is working.'

The rabbi said, 'Good, good. Now, I need you to do me a *mitzvah*, a favour. A friend is going on holiday, just for a few days. He needs someone to look after his dog. I suggested you. The dog will come tomorrow.'

'But Rabbi …' protested the husband, too late as the connection was broken.

The dog was not a small dog, but an old spaniel who farted a lot and slept a lot, everywhere.

Soon everyone was complaining. But no one wanted to be the one who left first. The dog barely crawled down the lanes and back again, panting heavily when a car forced them into the hedges.

The rabbi himself rang two nights later. 'Thank you, for this kindness. I need another *mitzvah* from you. My good friend has just had some bad news. She needs to leave her cat overnight. She lives near you. I suggested she should bring the cat round in the morning. Someone will be in?'

'Yes, Rabbi,' answered the husband. 'Good, good,' said the rabbi and rang off before more could be said.

Well, the cat arrived in its basket. Everyone knew it couldn't be allowed out because it didn't know the area. It was a feisty large cat who looked at everyone with slit eyes. It liked sleeping a lot, too. Unfortunately, it liked sleeping where the dog was. The dog, disgruntled at being moved, farted even more, and climbed on the pull-out bed. Her parents said it was about time they had the bedroom and his parents could sleep with the dog. The children ran round screaming at the dog, the cat, the grandparents. They were too excited to sleep. The wife went to bed with an icepack on her head. The man fell asleep in the children's room sat on the floor.

At the end of the next day, he rang the rabbi. 'Rabbi, my head is bursting.'

'Good, good,' said the rabbi. 'The cat is being collected in the morning, the dog in the afternoon. I suggest you thank your parents and parents-in-law and say you would love to see them all next Passover. They'll jump at the chance to go home at the same time.'

When all had gone in a flurry of kisses and farts, the children ate and went to bed early in their own rooms. The husband sat down with his wife. They ate, shared a bottle of wine and enjoyed the peace and quiet of the sea surging on the sand.

'Ah, what a space we have,' said the husband. 'Who said this house was cramped? It's a palace.'

Glossary

a bisl	*Yiddish* a little bit
afikomen	*Hebrew* the last bit of *matza* eaten at the *seder* meal on the first night of Passover before grace after meals is said
alephbeis	*Hebrew* Ashkenazi pronunciation alphabet
amidah	*Hebrew* the standing prayer central to all three daily services, at the end of which three steps are taken backwards and then three forwards
arba kanfot	*Hebrew* four-cornered vest worn by males under clothes with fringes on each corner to remind Jews of God's presence
aron hakodesh	*Hebrew* Holy Ark where the Torah scrolls are kept in a synagogue on the wall facing Jerusalem, usually east
Ashkenazi	*Hebrew* Jews who originated in Eastern Europe
baltefila	*Hebrew* Reader, leader of the service
baltekea	*Hebrew* one who blows the ram's horn, *shofar*
bar mitzvah	*Hebrew* when a boy assumes adult responsibility at 13
beis olom	*Hebrew* cemetery – literally, 'house of eternal rest'
bench/benched	*Yiddish* saying/said grace after meals
bimah	*Hebrew* platform in the synagogue where the reading desk is usually situated and the prayers are led from
bris/brit	*Hebrew* circumcision. A male Jew is circumcised at 8 days old, receiving his Hebrew name during the ceremony
broygus	*Yiddish* argument
bubbemeise/s	*Yiddish* fairy tale/s, old wives' tale/s
chad gadya	*Hebrew* an only kid, song from the Passover *seder*
Challah/challot/Khallah/khallot	
	Hebrew Plaited bread used on Shabbat. Often enriched with eggs. Two loaves are placed on the table under a *challah* cloth on Friday night waiting until after the

☙

	blessing over wine and people have washed their hands, saying a blessing, before they are uncovered and the blessing over bread is said. One loaf is cut and salt shaken over it before handing round for everyone to take a piece. Symbolising the gift of manna in the wilderness
charoset	*Hebrew* Ashkenazi version is a mixture of grated apple, ground almonds, cinnamon and kiddush wine. It looks like the mortar used by the Children of Israel to build the pyramids when they were slaves in Egypt. It is only eaten/used on Passover during the *seder*
chazan	*Hebrew* singer who leads the service in synagogue
chazer markt	*Yiddish* pig market, slang for a hiring fair
cheder	*Hebrew/Yiddish* Hebrew and religious school. Usually Sunday mornings and after secular school
Chelmnik	*Yiddish* a person from Chelm, the village of fools
cherem	*Hebrew* ban, shun, excommunicate
Chevra Kadisha	*Hebrew* holy brotherhood, the group that look after the dead and the dying
chometz	*Hebrew* non-Passover goods containing wheat, this includes dishes used during the rest of the year
chosan/khatan	*Hebrew* bridegroom
chrein	*Yiddish* grated raw horseradish with beetroot relish
chuppah/khuppa	*Hebrew* bridal canopy, with four wooden poles and a cloth canopy, often a *tallit* or embroidered velvet, symbolises the home the couple will make together. Everyone concerned in the ceremony stands under the canopy. If a new *sefer* Torah is being brought to the synagogue, it is paraded under a *chuppah* as if a bride coming to her new home
daven	*Yiddish* to say the prayers of the daily services, morning, afternoon and evening
farstunkene	*Yiddish* stinking, rotten
fis	*Yiddish* foot
gabbai	*Aramaic* treasurer of the synagogue
gam zeh letova	*Hebrew* this is also for good
gefilte fish	*Yiddish* minced fish, traditionally a white fish like cod, hake, whiting minced with onion, some add carrots and sugar, others salt, and then formed into balls and either boiled or fried
gelt	*Yiddish* money. Traditionally Hanukah *gelt* is given to children after the candles are lit. These days often given as chocolate money
Gemara	*Hebrew* after the Mishnah was published, it was

	studied exhaustively by generations of rabbis in both Babylonia and Israel. From 200–500CE, additional commentaries on the Mishnah were compiled and put together as the Gemara
get/gittin	*Hebrew* divorce/s
gilgul	*Hebrew* the soul of a dead person who passes into another living body to atone for past sins
goldene medina	*Yiddish* golden land/state usually referring to the USA
haggada/haggadot	*Hebrew* the traditional story of the Exodus read on the first night of Passover
hallel	*Hebrew* the set of psalms used in the festival prayers
hamotzi	*Hebrew* blessing over bread

Hanukah/Chanukah/Hanukka/Chanukkah

	Hebrew Festival commemorating the rededication of the Second Temple in Jerusalem after the Maccabbean Revolt against the Seleucid Empire. It celebrates the Jews' struggle for religious freedom. Also known as the Festival of Lights. It last eight days from 25th Kislev, which falls around November/ December. When they came to relight the *menorah* in the Temple they found only one sealed cruse of oil with enough to last for one day. The miracle was that the oil lasted for eight days. Food fried in oil is traditional. The *menorah* or *hanukkiah* is lit each evening starting from one candle on the first night, two on the second and so on.
HaShem	*Hebrew* The Name – a way of speaking of God without saying God, thereby not taking the name of God in vain, the third commandment, inadvertently.
havdalah	*Hebrew*– literally, 'separation' or 'division'. The ceremony takes place an hour after sunset on a Saturday night, when three stars are visible in the sky. The havdalah candle is a single candle with plaited wicks, a cup of wine and a box of spices. The candle is lit, the first fire after Shabbat has ended showing the separation between the holy day of Shabbat and the mundane ordinary week. The wine is blessed and passed around and the spices are blessed and passed to keep the sweet smell of Shabbat with us for the rest of the week
kaddish	*Aramaic* lit holy, the Aramaic prayer said when in mourning first at the graveside then during normal prayers if there is a *minyan*, a quorum of ten. Often

	said for the first year after a death then on the *yahrzeit*, anniversary of the death of a parent, spouse or child. Traditionally said by sons. If no sons, then sons-in-law on behalf of daughters.
kalle	*Hebrew* bride
kasher/kashering	*Hebrew* to prepare meat and poultry by soaking and salting to drain all blood before cooking. Jews are forbidden to eat blood of any kind, including sucking on a cut finger.
kelalah	*Hebrew* curse
keynahora	*Hebrew* avert the evil eye
khokhum	*Hebrew* wise person. When used in Yiddish it is ironic.
kiddush	*Hebrew* sanctification over wine on Shabbat, Friday night and Saturday after the service. On Saturdays this is often followed by sharing food.
kishke	*Yiddish* intestines
klaf/im	*Hebrew* paper, sheet. Used here to mean the paper inside a *mezuzah*. This is often more expensive than the outer case because of the work in writing the texts
klezmer	*Yiddish* music played by the folk musicians who travelled around for weddings, funerals, festivals, etc, in Eastern Europe
kosher	*Hebrew* Lawful, allowed, permitted
kreplach	*Yiddish* meat-filled pastry pockets that are either boiled or fried and added to soup a bit like ravioli
krikhn	*Yiddish* to crawl
kugel	*Yiddish* a baked pudding or casserole made from eggs and potato or *lokshn* (noodles). Usually made for Shabbat or *yomtov* as it is kept warm easily overnight.
kvell	*Yiddish* to express pride in family or friends and their accomplishments. In the sense of gushing with pride.
lachs	*Yiddish* salmon
lashonhora/ lashon hara	
	Hebrew badmouthing
latke/s	*Yiddish* Grated potato pancakes, like a *rosti*, tradition- ally eaten on Hanukah because they are fried in oil.
l'chayim	*Hebrew* To life! Traditional cheer.
ledor vador	*Hebrew* From generation to generation
lobos	*Yiddish*, especially British Yiddish a scamp, or rapscallion, someone, usually a boy who gets up to mischief.
lokshn	*Yiddish* noodles
lox	*Yiddish* smoked salmon

maggid	*Hebrew* itinerant preacher and teacher
makshefa	*Hebrew* witch
malakh hamoves	*Hebrew* angel of death
mantl	*Yiddish* overcoat
Ma'oz tzur	*Hebrew* thirteenth-century poem sung after the candles are lit during the festival of Hanukah.
mazal	*Hebrew* luck
mazal tov	*Hebrew* congratulations
mechaye	*Yiddish* something delicious, delightful, enjoyable
mechaye nefashos	*Yiddish* lit reviving souls extra delicious
mechutn	*Hebrew* related by marriage, as in the parents of your son-in-law
menorah	*Hebrew* Seven branched candelabra that stood in the Temple in Jerusalem as a symbol of God's presence. Also the nine-branched candlestick that is used during the festival of Hanukah to commemorate the rededication of the Temple. This type of *menorah* is often called a *hanukkiah* these days to distinguish it from the seven-branched one.
mentsch	*Yiddish* a person, a real gentleman, someone you'd aspire to be like
mezuzah/mezuzot	*Hebrew* The casing on a Jew's door on the right-hand side as commanded in Exodus, holds a prayer and the text of the Shema from Exodus. Some believe it protects the house. Any weathering of the handwritten scroll inside renders it invalid.
Midrash	*Hebrew* an ancient commentary on part of the Hebrew scriptures, attached to the biblical text. The earliest Midrashim come from the second century ad, although much of their content is older.
mikveh	*Hebrew* ritual bath, total immersion in water, living water, i.e. rainwater or seawater, not from a tap.
minyan	*Hebrew* quorum of ten men needed so certain prayers can be said in Orthodox Judaism or just a quorum of ten people.
Mishnah	*Hebrew* The Mishnah is the oral law in Judaism, as opposed to the written Torah, or the Mosaic Law. The Mishnah was collected and committed to writing about ce 200 and forms part of the Talmud. A particular teaching within the Mishnah is called a *midrash*.
mitzvah	*Hebrew* good deed, lit commandment
mohel	*Hebrew* person trained to circumcise a Jewish male at

	8 days old
ner tamid	*Hebrew* eternal light, hangs in front of the holy ark in the synagogue as a symbol that God's presence in constantly with us.
nigun	*Hebrew* wordless tune sung in praise of God
ohel	*Hebrew* lit. a hall. Usually on its own means the room at the cemetery where the coffin rests and prayers said before burial
omer	*Hebrew* A forty-nine-day liturgical season, originally a harvest festival, from the second day of Passover to the first day of Shavuot, during which marriages are prohibited and signs of mourning are observed.
oneg shabbat	*Hebrew* celebration of the Sabbath on a Friday night or more usually on a Saturday afternoon with songs, a lecture, discussions and food.
oy vey	*Yiddish* oh woe, oh dear!
Pesach	*Hebrew* Passover, festival of freedom
pesachdik	*Yiddish* things that are used on/for Passover
pilpel	*Hebrew* pepper, with the meaning of a spicy argument during learning
pupikl	*Yiddish* stomach of a chicken
Rebbe	*Yiddish* rabbi, a learned leader of community
Rosh Hashonnah	*Hebrew* Jewish New Year, a solemn time of year when Jews look back over the year and try to look forward to a better year
schmear	*Yiddish* smear, spread
schnorrer	*Yiddish* beggar
seder	*Hebrew* lit. order, the meal on the first night of Passover telling the story of the Exodus of the children of Israel from Egyptian slavery.
sedra/sidra	*Hebrew* Weekly portion of the Torah. The five books of Moses are divided into *sidrot*, portions that are read on Monday, Thursday and Shabbat mornings during the service. They are read in continuous order from the first Bereshit, Genesis until the last in Devarim, Deuteronomy. Each *sedra* has an appropriate portion from the rest of the Tanakh as its *haphtorah*, supplement to the Torah.
sefer	*Hebrew* book
sefer/sifrei Torah	*Hebrew* scroll/s of the Law
Sephardi	*Hebrew* Jews who originated in Western Europe, Spain, Portugal and the North Africa
Shabbos/Shabbes/ Shabbat	*Hebrew* Sabbath. Friday night to Saturday

night, sunset to an hour after sunset. Orthodox Jews do no work on this day.

shakharit/shacharis | *Hebrew* Morning prayers said with or without a *minyan*. The male puts on his *tallit* and his *tefillin* to say these prayers.

shalom | *Hebrew* Peace. Also used as a greeting like hello/goodbye

shalom aleichem | *Hebrew* Peace be upon you, Greeting one Jew gives another. The response is aleichem shalom (upon you peace).

shammas | *Hebrew* Servant candle used to light the other candles in a *menorah* or *hanukkiah* during Hanukah. This is so one light can light all the others without having to relight in between as a match goes out. So the blessing just said is over all the lights not just the first ones. It stands apart or in front of the other eight candles.

shammes | *Hebrew* servant of the synagogue who would go around waking up men for the morning service and collect them again for the afternoon and evening services and any other time a quorum is needed.

shayla/sheilah | *Hebrew* question, a religious question asked of a rabbi, whose answer must be implemented.

sheitel | *Yiddish* wig, specifically the wig a married woman wears to keep her own hair for her husband's eyes only.

Shekinah/ Shekhinah | *Hebrew* God's Presence, in Kabbalistic terms the Shekhinah is the feminine aspect of God

Shema | *Hebrew* Lit: Hear or Listen. The first word of the first line of the central tenet of Jewish belief recited morning and evening. Hear O Israel, the Eternal is our God, the Eternal is One. Also said when about to die.

shidduch | *Yiddish* arranged marriage

shiva | *Hebrew* seven-day mourning period. The mourners sit on the floor or low chairs when people come to pay their condolences. Services are held in the house so the mourners can say *kaddish*.

shochet | *Hebrew* ritual slaughterer of fowl and kosher animals

shtiebl | *Yiddish* prayer room in a residential house

shtreimel | *Yiddish* fur-brimmed hat worn by Polish Jews on holidays

shul | *Yiddish* synagogue

siddur	*Hebrew* prayer book
simcha/s	*Hebrew* celebration, joyous occasion like a wedding or *barmitzvah*
Simchat Torah	*Hebrew* Rejoicing of the Law. The festival of Simchat Torah celebrates the reading of the last portion and the beginning again of the first.
sof sof	*Hebrew* finally, eventually
sofer	*Hebrew* Scribe. A *sofer* is trained on how to prepare parchment, to cut quill pens, to grind ink as well as how to form the Hebrew letters with the correct ornamentation. A scribe is highly prized. It takes many hours to write even one paragraph of a Torah scroll.
takke	*Yiddish* really, truly
tallit/tallis	*Hebrew* prayer shawl with fringes on all four corners usually white with black stripes but sometimes blue stripes instead.
Talmud	*Hebrew* the body of Jewish civil and ceremonial law and legend comprising the Mishnah and the Gemara. There are two versions of the Talmud: the Babylonian Talmud (which dates from the fifth century ad but includes earlier material) and the earlier Palestinian or Jerusalem Talmud.
Tanakh	*Hebrew* The Bible. Acronym: T = Torah (the Five books of Moses: Genesis, Exodus, Leviticus, Numbers, Deuteronomy) N = Nevi'im (Prophets containing Joshua, Judges, Samuel I, II, Kings I, II, Isaiah, Jeremiah, Ezekiel, and the Twelve Minor Prophets) Kh = Ketuvim (Writings containing Psalms, Proverbs, Job, Song of Songs, Ruth, Lamentations, Ecclesiastes, Esther, Daniel, Ezra, Nehemiah, Chronicles I, II).
tati	*Yiddish* dad
tchatchke/s	*Yiddish* a small ornament, decorative only.
tefillin	*Hebrew* phylacteries. There are two, one for the head, one for the arm. Both have a black box that has handwritten scrolls within with texts from Exodus and Deuteronomy. The head one has two leather straps that hold it on the head over the temple and then hang down the back. The arm one is placed on the upper left arm, where the box is positioned facing the heart, and then the single strap is wound down the left arm and round the palm and fingers.

During the morning prayers the strap is wound and
rewound to form Hebrew letters over the palm and
fingers. *Tefillin* are worn only during the morning
prayers.

treifah	*Yiddish* unclean, non-permitted
tzaddik/tzaddikim	*Hebrew* saint/s
tzedaka	*Hebrew* charity
tzedek	*Hebrew* justice
tzitzit	*Hebrew* fringes, either on the corners of the *arba kanfot* or *tallit* as specified in Exodus
tzores	*Hebrew* troubles
uisge	*Scots Gaelic* whisky
vigdis	*Yiddish* lullaby
yahrzeit/yohrzeit	*Yiddish* anniversary of the day of someone's death
yeshiva bocher	*Hebrew* boy/man who studies Torah at a Hebrew academy
yeshiva/ot	*Hebrew* place where the study of the Torah is the only concern
yiskor	*Hebrew* memorial prayer for lost loved ones said in the synagogue on the festivals of Pesach, Shavuos, Succos and especially Yom Kippur
Yom Kippur	*Hebrew* Day of Atonement, holiest day in the Jewish calendar, ten days after Rosh Hashonnah, a fast of twenty-five hours, no food or drink, contemplating and repenting all the sins committed during the year and hoping for a better year usually spent praying in the synagogue.
zayde, zeide	*Yiddish* grandfather
zieskeit	*Yiddish* sweeting, sweetheart
zuzim	*Aramaic* coins worth less than a penny

CONTRIBUTORS

Alexander Knapp	London
Anthony Fagin	Cornwall
Anthony Joseph	Birmingham/London
Del Reid	London
Doreen Brellisford	Liverpool
Ella Newman	Liverpool
Fay Phillips	Manchester
Harvey Kurzfield	Cornwall
Jeremy Jacobson	Cornwall
John Minkes	Cardiff
June Kendal	Liverpool
June Wood	Liverpool
Leslie Lipert	Cornwall
Marie Slott	Liverpool
Marilyn Bracey	Liverpool
Michael Adler	Manchester
N. Rappaport	Manchester
Neil Cooper	Birmingham/London
Pearl Rayner	Liverpool
Rabbi Maurice Michaels	Bournemouth/London
Rita Austin	Manchester
Rudi Leavor	Bradford
Rufus	Liverpool
S. Ellman	Manchester
Shirley Baker	Liverpool
Shirley Selsdon	Bournemouth
Stephen Jaffe	Belfast
Sybil Abrams	Liverpool

THANKS TO MY BETA READERS:

Helen Northey
Sue Field
Toni Berg
Yvonne Stevens

BIBLIOGRAPHY

Azar, Francois and Bouloubasis, Petros, *Bewitched by Solika and other Judeo-Spanish Tales* (Lior editions, 2016)

Ben-Amos, Dan (ed.), *Folktales of the Jews Vol. 1 Tales from The Sephardic Dispersion* (The Jewish Publication Society, Philadelphia, 2006)

Ben-Amos, Dan (ed.), *Folktales of the Jews Vol. 2 Tales from Eastern Europe* (The Jewish Publication Society, Philadelphia, 2007)

Ben-Amos, Dan (ed.), *Folktales of the Jews Vol. 3 Tales from Arab Lands* (The Jewish Publication Society, Philadelphia, 2011)

Bermant, Chaim, *The Cousinhood* (Eyre & Spottiswoode, 1971)

Collins, Dr Kenneth E., *Scotland's Jews: A Guide to the History and Community of the Jews in Scotland*, 2nd ed. (Scottish Council of Jewish Communities, 2008)

Daiches, David, *Two Worlds Promised Lands* (Canongate Classics, 1997)

Elswit, Sharon, *The Jewish Story Finder* (McFarlan & Company Inc., 2009)

Englander, David (ed.), *A Documentary History of Jewish Immigrants in Britain 1840–1920* (Leicester University Press, 1994)

Gilbert, Martin, *The Dent Atlas of Jewish History from 2000 BCE to the Present Day* (Dent Ltd, 1993)

Hadas. Moses (trans.), *Fables of a Jewish Aesop* (David R. Godine Publisher, 2001)

Lachs, Vivi, *Whitechapel Noise: Jewish Immigrant Life in Yiddish Song and Verse London 1884–1914* (Wayne State University Press, 2018)

Mloter, Eleanor & Joseph, *Songs of Generations New Pearls of Yiddish Song* (The Workmen's Circle, New York, 2004)

Pearce, Keith, *The Jews of Cornwall, A History* (Halsgrove, 2014)

Reid, Derek, *Six Yiddish Street Songs of East London: Proceedings of First International Conference on Jewish Music* (City University of London, 1994)

Roth, Rita, *The Power of Song and Other Sephardic Tales*, (The Jewish
    Publication Society, Philadelphia, 2007)

Samuel, Edgar, *At the End of the Earth: Essays on the History of the Jews in
    England and Portugal* (The Jewish Historical Society of England, 2004)

Schram, Peninah, *Stories within Stories from the Jewish Oral Tradition*
    (Jason Aronson Inc., 2000)

Schram, Peninah, *Jewish Stories One Generation Tells Another* (Jason
    Aronson Inc., 1989)

Schwartz, Howard, *Leaves from the Garden of Eden 100 Classic Jewish Tales*
    (Oxford University Press, 2009)

Schwartz, Howard, *Tree of Souls: The Mythology of Judaism* (Oxford
    University Press, 2004)

Schwartz, Howard, *Miriam's Tambourine: Jewish Folk Tales from around
    the World* (Oxford Paperbacks, 1988)

Sherman, Josepha, *Rachel the Clever and other Jewish Folktales* (August
    House Inc., 1993)

Taylor, Marilyn, *Faraway Home* (O'Brien, 2018)

Teman, Elly, *The Red String: The Cultural History of a Jewish Folk Symbol,
    Jewish Cultural Studies vol. 1* (Littman Library of Jewish Civilization,
    Oxford, 2008)

Williams, Bill, *Jewish Manchester: An illustrated History* (DB publishing,
    2014)

Jewish Historical Studies vol. 31 1988–1990 (The Jewish Historical
    Society, 1990)

Jewish Historical Studies vol. 34 1994–1996 (The Jewish Historical
    Society, 1997)

Jewish Historical Studies vol. 36 *1999–2001* (The Jewish Historical
    Society, 2001)

Jewish Historical Studies vol. 40 (The Jewish Historical Society, 2005)

Jewish Historical Studies vol. 42 (The Jewish Historical Society, 2009)

Jewish Historical Studies vol. 43 (The Jewish Historical Society, 2011)

WEBSITES

http://digital-library.qub.ac.uk/digital/collection/p15979coll24/id/97/
    rec/2

http://ww1hull.org.uk/index.php/
    hull-and-the-first-world-war/133-hull-s-jewish-community

www.norwichsynagogue.org.uk

www.plymouthsynagogue.com

www.sacred-texts.com/jud/loj/index.htm

www.sephardifolklit.org

https://bradfordjewish.org.uk

https://jewishmuseum.ie

https://jewishmuseum.org.uk

https://jhse.org

www.jewishcork.com

www.jewishgen.org/jcr-uk/susser/thesis

www.liverpoolmuseums.org.uk/mol/visit/documents/Liverpool-Jewish-community-trail.pdf

www.manchesterjewishmuseum.com

www.scojec.org

www.belfastjewishcommunity.org.uk

www.british-history.ac.uk/vch/warks/vol8/pp480-489#p37

www.garnethill.org.uk

www.jewisheastend.com

www.jewishencyclopedia.com

www.jewishgen.org/jcr-uk

www.jewishireland.org

www.jtrails.org.uk

www.leedsjewishcommunity.com

www.theglasgowstory.com